A Christmas Carol

A musical to raise the spirits

☙

BOOK & LYRICS BY
Chris Blackwood

MUSIC BY
Piers Chater Robinson

BASED ON THE NOVEL BY
Charles Dickens

First Edition Published in 2010
Reprinted in 2011 and 2012 by
International Theatre & Music Ltd
Garden Studios
71–75 Shelton Street
Covent Garden
London
WC2H 9JQ
Tel: + 44 (0)20 7470 8786
www.itmshows.com

Printed and bound in the UK by Biddles, part of the
MPG Books Group, Bodmin and King's Lynn

ISBN 978-0-9565719-0-8

www.AChristmasCarolMusical.co.uk

A Christmas Carol

Book and Lyrics by Chris Blackwood

Music by Piers Chater Robinson

CAST

DICKENS   *doubling as 1st Gentleman, Schoolmaster, Fezziwig's Fiddler, Fred's Party Guest & Businessman 1*

EBENEZER SCROOGE

BOB CRATCHIT

MRS CRATCHIT   *doubling as Mrs Fezziwig & Mrs Dilber*

FRED   *doubling as Young Scrooge*

BELLE   *doubling as Beth & Mrs Filch*

JACOB MARLEY   *doubling as Mr Fezziwig & Businessman 3*

The Ghosts

CHRISTMAS PAST   *doubling as 2nd Gentleman & Businessman 2*

CHRISTMAS PRESENT   *doubling as Old Joe*

CHRISTMAS YET TO COME   *Non-speaking*

The Cratchit Children: *Martha, Peter, Belinda, Tiny Tim*

Ensemble of street urchins, debtors, stall holders, party guests etc.

A Christmas Carol

Musical Numbers

★ ★ ★

ACT I

1. Prologue/Christmas Cheer/Ebenezer Scrooge . . . . Cast
2. Shillings, Pounds and Pence . . . . Scrooge, Fred & Cratchit
3. Good Things Come . . . . Cratchit, Tiny Tim & Cast
4. Reprise – Ebenezer Scrooge . . . . Scrooge
5. Link by Link . . . . Marley, Scrooge & Tortured Souls
6. Shine a Light . . . . Christmas Past
6a. Incidental Music . . . . Scrooge's Schooldays
7. The Pride of the Ball . . . . The Fezziwigs & Guests
8. Heart of Gold . . . . Belle
8a. Incidental Music . . . . Belle and Young Ebenezer's Parting
9. Remember . . . . Young Scrooge & Scrooge
10. Drink it In . . . . Christmas Present, Scrooge & Cast

ACT II

11. Entr'acte . . . . Dickens
12. Reprise – Good Things Come . . . . Cast
13. Do as the Cratchits Do . . . . The Cratchit Family
14. God Bless . . . . The Cratchit Children & Children of London
14a. Incidental Dance Music . . . . Fred's Party
15. Am I That Man? . . . . Scrooge
16. Just Desserts . . . . Old Joe, Mrs Dilber & Mrs Filch
16a. Incidental Music . . . . The Graveyard
17. Turn Back the Clock . . . . Scrooge
18. The Man is Mad . . . . Scrooge, Mrs Dilber & Mrs Filch
19. Finale . . . . Scrooge & Cast
20. Bows
21. Playout

ACT I

An icy blue mist floats across an empty stage. A moon can be seen on the cyclorama. We hear footsteps echoing along a cobbled street and through the mist appears the owner of the footsteps walking towards the front of the stage. As his silhouette is seen, we hear the slow chime of a clock and a Roman numeric clock face is seen appearing on the face of the moon. The lone figure is CHARLES DICKENS.

MUSIC CUE 1. PROLOGUE/CHRISTMAS CHEER/EBENEZER SCROOGE – CAST

Music starts underscoring. Dickens comes to a halt and speaks clearly. He is the Dickens of all the pictures we know; he is a benevolent and fatherly figure. General note, this libretto gives an indication of who sings what and when, so in rehearsals please see the score for the exact vocal pattern.

DICKENS   Once upon a time … For time is all we have, and how we choose to use it is our own business but remember, time is precious. You can't own it, but you can use it. You can't keep it, but you can spend it. And once you've lost it you can never, ever, get it back.

A lamplighter drags a solitary lamp onto the stage and reaches his pole to light it.

But … what if you were given a second chance to live your life again? What choices would you make? This is the story of a gentleman who is given that chance. A chance to change what went before, a chance to make amends. A chance to turn back the clock. Once upon a time …

LAMPLIGHTER   *Five o'clock and all's well*

DICKENS   Once upon a time – of all the good days in the year …

LAMPLIGHTER   *Five o'clock and all's well*
Five o'clock and all's well
Five o'clock and all's well

A brazier is seen through the fog. A number of ragged youths and men stand round it, warming their hands.

RAGGED YOUTHS   *Blimey, it's parky*
Blimey, it's cold

> *We're like brass monkeys*
> *If truth be told*

DICKENS   Once upon a time – of all the good days of the year – on Christmas Eve, when the bleak alleyways of London were bedecked with holly sprigs and berries which crackled in the lamp-heat of the shops and stalls …

A young lad with a lamp runs across the way towards a man and woman holding out his hand

LAMP LAD   *Light your way, sir,*
Light your way, sir
For a penny

They shoo the boy away. He looks about him for another potential customer.

LAMPLIGHTER   *Five o'clock and all's well (etc please see score)*

The Lamp Lad runs toward Dickens and stops, holding out his hand once more.

LAMP LAD   *Light your way, sir,*
Light your way, sir
For a penny

Dickens smiles and laughs, giving the boy a penny from his waistcoat.

DICKENS   Merry Christmas, boy.

LAMP LAD   *God Bless you, Guv'nor*
May you be blessed
You're one in a million
Not like all the rest

The boy runs off into the fog, as the ensemble sing their various calls in counterpoint.

DICKENS   The gruff old bell in the ancient church struck the hours and the quarters in the clouds as if its teeth were chattering in its frozen head.

RAGGED YOUTHS *Blimey, it's parky*
Blimey, it's cold
We're like brass monkeys
If truth be told

DICKENS	And although the weather was cold, bleak and biting and the people were wheezing up and down beating their hands upon their breasts and stamping their feet on the pavement stones to warm them, their hearts were full of Christmas cheer.

A gentleman scurries across past the lamplighter.

LAMPLIGHTER	*Five o'clock and all's well*
GENTLEMAN	Pardon me, I can't help but notice that you have been calling five for quite some time now. Surely it must be later.
LAMPLIGHTER	That's right, sir, but I only get paid by the hour.
	Five o'clock and all's well
DICKENS	Every single man with joy in his heart, a spring in his step and, above all, a desire to spread good will, for one day at least in the whole three hundred and sixty-five days of the year.

A number of lit barrows are pulled on and the sides of the buildings in the street are seen. With lights glowing from windows and the barrows, the stage starts to brighten in the evening glow of lamps. A stall with wrapped steam puddings

PUDDING MAN	*Come see the wares we proudly show* *Our festive Christmas grub*
WOMAN	*I tried his figgy pudding once* *And now I'm in the club*
VARIOUS	*Your final chance to make this Christmas* *What it ought to be* *Filled with peace and goodwill and harmony* *Peace and goodwill* *Filled with hope and peace and generosity*

A poulterer stops a large woman and her small husband and waves a large goose by the neck at them.

POULTERER	*A stately goose fit for a king* *We always sell the best*

LARGE WOMAN   *Just take a look, it's just the thing*

HUSBAND   *A plump and ample breast*

The woman grabs him by the scruff and drags him to another stall.

ALL   *Your final chance to make this Christmas*
What it ought to be
Filled with peace and goodwill and harmony
Peace and goodwill
Filled with hope and peace and generosity

LAMPLIGHTER   *Five o'clock and all's well*

Out of the crowd comes a small man, who lifts his cap to the ladies politely and smiles. He hurries towards Scrooge's office. This is BOB CRATCHIT, an amiable man, over-worked and flustered, he is only truly at home with his family and friends.

SAM   Bob Cratchit! I'm surprised the old miser let him out at this time of day.

WOMAN   It's Christmas Eve.

SAM   You think old Scrooge cares what day it is? You don't know him very well do you? *(To Bob, as he passes)* Bob.

BOB   Mr Billickin.

SAM   *(joking)* Mr Scrooge give you time off for Christmas shopping?

BOB   We've been at the stock exchange all day. I'm to get back quick sharp and make sure the books are balanced before I go home tonight.

WOMAN   But it's five o'clock already …

BOB   Nevertheless, Mr Scrooge likes everything in its place …

WOMAN   But it's Christmas …

BOB   All the more reason to get it done and get it done quickly so Good Day to you both and Merry Christmas.

BOTH   Merry Christmas to you, Bob.

Bob hurries into the office.

WOMAN	Poor man.
SAM	You can say that again.
WOMAN	You know, I think it's time to be getting home. Don't want to catch me death on Christmas Eve.
SAM	We'll have snow before the day is out. Mark my words.

> *I didn't think this day could get much colder*
> *And all I have to show for it is I'm a little older*
> *Though the winter chills me to the bone*
> *And ice is turning water now to stone*
> *I have the very thing to warm my heart*
> *For Christmas time is now about to start*
> *So*

CHORUS	*Don't give a fig about the weather*
	Come sing; the time is near
	Come sing a little song together
	Fill the air with Christmas cheer
WOMEN	*Don't sing about the bitter bleakness, frosty and cold*
	Christmas will bring a little weakness in young and old
MEN	*Take out the mistletoe and this'll be the time for a kiss*
	Who could beget a better reason in the season of bliss
ALL	*Sing a yuletide greeting*
	Just one day each year
	Though it may be fleeting
	Make the time for Christmas cheer
FAT MAN	*Goose with tons of trimming*
VENDOR	*Port wine, brandy, beer*
DRUNK	*Oh, my head is swimming!*
VENDOR	*That's the spirit*
ALL	*Christmas cheer*

The drunk makes a number of attempts to take money from his pocket. In the end he places one hand over his eye, takes out the money and waves it in the vendor's face.

VENDOR	Something I can get for you, sir?

DRUNK	I'd like something icy and full of gin
VENDOR	(*shouting*) Doris, someone to see you, love.

A buxom lady (Doris) grabs the drunk lustily and whirls into a dance as the others join in. Dance section.

ALL	***Ring out the bells of love and laughter***
	Joy has no equal here
	Chime for now and ever after
	Sounding forth the Christmas cheer
	Deck out the halls with all the jollity and joking and jest
	Fill ev'ry stocking with a shocking lot of love and the rest
	Let us be cheery 'stead of weary, 'stead of gloomy and glum
	Come raise a glass to present, past and all the things yet to come
	Goodwill, peace on earth to
	All those far or near
	All this I would wish you
	Wrapped up in this Christmas cheer

Through the crowds, waving his stick to clear the way, comes EBENEZER SCROOGE, a man who lowers the already sub zero temperature with his presence. A stiffened gaited, pointed nosed, blue lipped, red-eyed skinflint.

SCROOGE	Out! Out of my way! Haven't you people got better things to do?
MAN	It's Christmas, Mr Scrooge.
SCROOGE	Bah! Humbug! Take yourselves from my doorstep or I shall have you all forcibly removed.
DICKENS	(*to the audience*) Oh, but he was tight-fisted old miser, Scrooge! A squeezing, wrenching, grasping, scraping, clutching, covetous old sinner!
SCROOGE	(*to Dickens*) Have you quite finished? I'm not deaf, you know.
MAN	***Blimey, he can hear us.***
WOMAN	***Frosty so-and-so!***
ALL	***Yes when Scrooge is near us***
	It's like eight degrees below

SCROOGE	This whole damned world is suffering from an appalling case of optimism but I have the cure.

Shall I tell you something wonderful and new
All about this precious time which causes much ado?
Scrimping for those pennies, spending come what may
And growing poorer in effect by every Boxing Day
Gluttonous and heaving, smacking at your lips
Adding extra inches to those ever growing hips
Creaking tables full of port, puddings, peaches, plums
Never thinking forward when you've naught to eat but crumbs
Who's the man who saves you when the debts to pay are huge?
Benevolent as always Mister Ebenezer Scrooge

POOR MAN	Could I have a moment of your time, Mr Scrooge?
SCROOGE	Time is money, sir, and you have already cost me a farthing. Out of my way!

Scrooge pushes him away with his stick and walks on only to stop a few steps away and spin on his heels.

	Wait! You owe me twenty pounds.
POOR MAN	Yes, sir, it was about that ...
SCROOGE	I want no sob story, man. The balance is due.
POOR MAN	I ... I cannot pay you, sir. My wife, you see, sir, is ill, sir ...
SCROOGE	Your wife's ill health is not my concern. My concern is what will become of my twenty pounds, sir.
POOR MAN	I... I don't know, sir, really I don't.
SCROOGE	Debts are to be paid on time. Read the small print.
POOR MAN	Give me more time, sir, I beg you.
SCROOGE	Time is something neither of us have. I run a business, sir, and it is not my business to let people like you fleece me out of all I own. Pay your debt in full or find yourself celebrating Christmas Day in prison, sir.
POOR MAN	But ...

SCROOGE	Good day.
POOR MAN	Please …
SCROOGE	*(with a finality)* Good day.

> *Bus'ness is my bus'ness, man is nought to me*
> *Let others smile and doth their caps and talk of charity*
> *Swift to pick my pocket when the rent is due*
> *But miserable pleaders when I turn the screw*
> *How's a man to profit? How's a man to thrive*
> *When they're grasping for my pennies, should I help the dogs survive?*
> *Frittr'ing all their earnings, wasting it away*
> *Have they any put aside to brave that rainy day?*
> *Well, here it comes, that stormy cloud, here's the big deluge*
> *Who'll save you drowning for a price? Ebenezer Scrooge*

ALL	*Debts are getting larger and his terms are bloomin' huge* *And the only one to profit*
SCROOGE	*Who?*
ALL	*Ebenezer*
MAN	*Nasty geezer*
ALL	*Ebenezer Scrooge*

Scrooge has opened the door to his office and turns in the doorway.

SCROOGE	Humbug!

Scrooge slams the door on the merrymakers. Quietly the merriment slowly starts anew.

ALL	*Don't let that jolly appetiser* *Spoil all that you hold dear* *Block out that melancholy miser* *Banish him with Christmas Cheer* *Take up the holly and be jolly, raise a glass, make a toast* *Stoke up the fire and retire to the place you love most* *London is stating that it's waiting for the festivity* *Wrap up the present, pluck the pheasant, let us trim up the tree*

Here's a Christmas wish
To all who you hold dear
Make this time delic- (delish)
-ious laden down with Christmas Cheer
One last time, (shouting) let's shout it
Sing out, let us hear
We won't go without it
Very Merry Christmas Cheer

MEN   *Very Merry Christmas Cheer*

WOMEN   *Very Merry Christmas*

MEN   *Very Merry Christmas*

WOMEN   *Very merry, very merry*

MEN   *Very merry, very merry*

ALL   *Very Merry Christmas Cheer*
                Very Merry Christmas Cheer

MUSIC CUE 1A. SCENE CHANGE UNDERSCORE

Tableau and play out as light cross-fades to Dickens as the merrymakers start to disperse or go back to what they were doing. Ragged youths turn the truck of Scrooge's office. The inside is dimly lit.

DICKENS   And although the merrymakers went about the frosty evening with enough warmth in their hearts to heat the houses of Parliament, it had no influence on Scrooge. No warmth could warm him, nor wintry weather chill him. No wind that blew was bitterer than he.

Scrooge is counting pennies into a lockbox, speedily and muttering figures to himself. Bob, still in his muffler, sits high on his stool above his clerk's desk, scribbling frantically in a large ledger with a quill. It tickles his nose and he sneezes.

SCROOGE   Keep sneezing like that and I shall dock your pay. I don't pay you to sneeze. Sneeze all you like in your own time. This is my time and I will not have sneezing.

BOB   Of course, sir. Sorry, Mr Scrooge, it's just my little fire seems to have gone out. Could I trouble you for ...

SCROOGE   Want, want, want! What is it about this time of year? Everyone wants something for nothing.

Scrooge moves to a large locked box. He takes out an enormous bunch of keys and selects one. He opens the box, making sure Bob does not see the contents.

SCROOGE   Hold out your hand.

Bob does so and Scrooge takes out a pair of tongs with which he holds a tiny piece of coal. He drops it into Bob's hand.

SCROOGE   And don't burn it too quickly. I'm not made of money. On second thoughts …

Scrooge grabs the coal with his tongs and snaps it back into his box.

SCROOGE   *(locking the box)* Use the candle.

Bob wanders, dejectedly, back to his desk. He lights his candle and warms his frozen hands before picking up his quill once more and scribbling as before. The door is flung open and Scrooge drops a penny on the floor beneath his desk. He scrabbles to find it. Fred appears, all in a glow; his face ruddy and handsome; his eyes sparkle with humour. He grins at Bob Cratchit who raises an eyebrow, surprised to see him.

FRED   Hi-ho! Still at work, Bob? What's to become of all the little Cratchits? Christmas postponed?

BOB   I should hope not, sir.

FRED   Scribbling when you should be merrymaking? Where's that old uncle of mine? I'll tell him a thing or two.

Bob points to below Scrooge's desk to direct Fred. Fred stands next to the desk and shouts.

            (cheerily) A merry Christmas, uncle! God save you!

Scrooge bangs his head on the desk as he jumps up. He has the penny in his hand.

SCROOGE   *(placing the penny in the box and slamming it shut)* Bah! Humbug!

FRED   *(with mock shock)* Christmas a humbug, uncle? You don't mean that, I am sure.

SCROOGE   *(locking the box and squirreling it away)* I do. Merry Christmas! What reason have you to be merry? You're poor enough.

FRED   Come, then. What right have you to be dismal? You're rich enough.

SCROOGE   (*he has no answer but ...*) Bah! Humbug.

FRED   Don't be cross, uncle.

MUSIC CUE 2. SHILLINGS, POUNDS AND PENCE – SCROOGE, FRED & BOB

SCROOGE   What else can I be when I live in such a world of fools as this? Merry Christmas! What's Christmas time to you but a time for paying bills without money and a time for finding yourself a year older, but not an hour richer? If there's one thing that makes me lose my usual good natured humour it's a man with a ruddy complexion spouting seasonal clap-trap!

I'm a gentleman who's gentle as a gentleman can be
The epitome of what you'd call respectability
I'm a man who's fairly frugal
And who's careful to a fault
And I think that I would class me
As a man who's worth his salt
But there's one thing that will put my humour into an eclipse
It's those lunatics who go about with Christmas on their lips
So take your season's greetings
And the joy that you dispense
Only one thing raises spirits and that's shillings pounds and pence
The only thing makes sense
Is shillings, pounds and pence
Take your stockings and go hang 'em
Hang those garlands on your fence
And go hang yourself and leave me to my shillings pounds and pence

SCROOGE   If I could work my will, every idiot who goes about with "Merry Christmas" on his lips, should be boiled with his own pudding, and buried with a stake of holly through his heart.

FRED   You are missing one of the most wonderful times of the year, Uncle. Come, spend it with me and my family.

SCROOGE	Family? One of the reasons I live alone!
SCROOGE	*Why must I be bothered by an endless family* *Full of grasping rotten apples falling from the family tree?* *They will tap you for a fiver* *They will squeeze you for a quid* *And swear blind each time you ask them* *That they're sure they never did* *They will live the life of Riley on the money that you earn* *They will borrow on your name as if they've got the cash to burn* *And when you're in the poorhouse* *For the miscreants' offence* *They'll be in the South of France* *With all your shillings, pounds and pence*
FRED	Uncle, surely you don't think that?
SCROOGE	I'm sure I do.
SCROOGE	*The only thing makes sense* *Is shillings, pounds and pence* *Relatively speaking* *Relations make me tense* *So, I'd rather spend an evening with my shillings, pounds and pence*
FRED	Uncle, I ask nothing of you. Why cannot we be friends? Come dine with my wife and me tomorrow.
SCROOGE	Wife? What possessed you to take a wife?
FRED	I fell in love.
SCROOGE	You fell in love! Fool. Saddled with another drain on your resources.
FRED	I love her.
SCROOGE	Women! Never a moment's peace! There is a reason why English is called the Mother Tongue, sir; Father never gets a chance to use it.

SCROOGE	*A wife is like a millstone that is hung about our necks*
	And her endless jibber-jabber turns us into nervous wrecks
	She'll want a brand new parlour
	And all that it entails
	With all the gaudy splendour
	That would shame the Prince of Wales
	And when she's spent a fortune, she will drive a man insane
	For she'll just decide it's not quite right and do it all again
	Pack her bags and hats and dresses
	Tell the woman 'Get thee hence'
	And keep your thieving fingers off
	My shillings, pounds and pence
SCROOGE	*The only thing makes sense*
	Is shillings, pounds and pence
	You'll find she's growing bigger
	With a figure that's immense
	And the only figures that I love are shillings, pounds and pence
	So take your Merry Christmas
	And stick it where you will
	Confounded love unbounded
	Is a thing that makes me ill
	You may call me what you like and you may laugh at my expense
	I'm the one who's sitting pretty on my
	Crowns and guineas, notes and pennies
	Florins, sovereigns, silver sixpence
	Shillings pounds and pence
SCROOGE	There, I have said my piece and let that be an end to it.
FRED	Uncle!
SCROOGE	Let me be!
FRED	Whatever you say, I am determined to give you joy of the season.
SCROOGE	Much good it has done you!
FRED	There are many things from which I might have derived good and by which I haven't profited, I daresay, Christmas

among them, but I've always thought of Christmas time as a good time; a kind, forgiving, charitable, pleasant time and, therefore, Uncle, though it has never put a scrap of gold in my pocket, I believe it *has* done me good and *will* do me good and I say, God bless it!

Bob applauds spontaneously and Scrooge whips around to fix him in his sight. Bob suddenly pretends that it was the cold that made him clap and continues to clap his arms and stamp his feet, blowing on his hands.

SCROOGE   Let me hear another sound from you and you'll celebrate Christmas by losing your job. (*To Fred*) You're quite a powerful speaker, sir, I wonder you don't go into Parliament.

Scrooge sits back at his ledger.

FRED   Uncle, come, will you dine with me tomorrow or no?

SCROOGE   I'd sooner find myself stoking the very fires of Hell.

FRED   I'll take that as a no, then. Well, I'm sorry to find you so resolute, but I'll keep my Christmas humour to the last so Merry Christmas, Uncle!

SCROOGE   Good afternoon!

FRED   And a Happy New Year.

Fred kisses Scrooge on the top of his head quickly which incenses the old man.

SCROOGE   Get out!

Fred leaves but turns in the doorway.

FRED   Merry Christmas, Bob!

BOB   A Merry Christmas to you, sir.

Scrooge eyes Bob malevolently from his ledger as Fred exits. Bob begins to scribble furiously at his desk. The clock strikes seven. Bob hurriedly grabs his coat and clears his desk. Scrooge looks up.

SCROOGE   That clock is fast.

Bob looks at him. Scrooge slams his ledger shut.

You'll be wanting all day tomorrow, I suppose?

BOB	If it's quite convenient, sir.
SCROOGE	It is not convenient and it's not fair.

Scrooge gets up and Bob grabs Scrooge's coat and starts to help him into it.

SCROOGE	If I was to stop you half a crown for it, you'd think yourself ill-used, I'll be bound?

Bob smiles weakly.

And yet, you don't think me ill-used when I pay a day's wages for no work.

BOB	It *is* only one day a year, sir.
SCROOGE	A poor excuse for picking a man's pocket every twenty-fifth of December!

Scrooge counts out a number of coins and places them into Bob's hand.

Be here all the earlier the following morning!

BOB	Of course, sir, thank you, sir. Merr—

Bob stops himself as Scrooge looks at him furiously. Bob scuttles out.

SCROOGE	(*muttering to himself*) There's another fellow! My clerk! Fifteen shillings a week, a wife and a clan of squealing brats and still he talks of a Merry Christmas! I'll retire to Bedlam, so I will! I'll find more sense!

A small voice is heard singing 'God Rest Ye Merry Gentlemen' outside the door. Scrooge takes up his cane, opens the door and chases the small boy away.

SCROOGE	Get away from me with that confounded caterwauling!

He turns to lock the door.

BOY	Where's your bloomin' Christmas spirit?
SCROOGE	(*turning sharply and waving his cane*) Here it is! Take care you don't feel it on your backside! Scoundrel!
BOY	Miserable old goat!
SCROOGE	Why you little ...

As he turns, Scrooge sees Sam Billikin smirking.

Samuel Billikin! (*taking out a small notebook and pencil*) How fortuitous!

SAM	(*instantly sober*) Ah, Mr Scrooge…
SCROOGE	Your debt is due. Five shillings.
SAM	It's been a bad week.
SCROOGE	A bad week? Since when does a chestnut seller have a bad week at Christmas?
SAM	I've been giving more credit than usual, sir. Some people can't afford …
SCROOGE	I do not lend money so that others can seem charitable, sir. That is a luxury neither myself nor you can afford. Five shillings!
SAM	Couldn't you extend a little kindness, sir?
SCROOGE	It will cost you two shillings more for the trouble.
SAM	But, Mr Scrooge …
SCROOGE	I could take your stall.
SAM	Two shillings it is then.
SCROOGE	A very astute business man.
SAM	Thank you, Mr Scrooge.

The boy returns and blows a raspberry at Scrooge and Scrooge sets off after him, waving his cane; the other vendors physically moving from him. Bob enters with Tiny Tim on his shoulder.

BOB	Well, Tim, my dear, what is it to be? Where shall we start?
TIM	Christmas isn't Christmas without a pudding, Pa.
BOB	You're right, my boy. But wait, what about the goose?
TIM	We need that as well.
BOB	A goose *and* a pudding! Well, it seems like we're going to have to toss a coin. Heads, the pudding; tails, the goose.
TIM	Don't lose it, Pa, or we'll have none at all.

BOB   Clever lad! What would your mother say if we came home empty-handed?

Bob tosses the coin and catches it. He looks at it.

Goose, it is then!

Tiny Tim looks a little down-hearted.

Goose first, pudding after!

Tim smiles and Bob lifts him aloft once more. They approach the Poulterer's stall.

POULTERER   (*smiling*) Mr Cratchit! Master Cratchit!

BOB   Show us your finest Goose, Mr Parry!

POULTERER   I've got birds that would make Her Majesty's table look bare.

BOB   I'm sure you have, Mr Parry, but consider the size of our table. What've you got for a shilling?

MUSIC CUE 3. GOOD THINGS COME

TIM   We *will* have a Merry Christmas, won't we, Pa?

BOB   *Good things come*
To those who wait
No matter who from me and you to heads of state
But all I know
This much is true
That all the good things now are bundled up in you
When you are near
My world's complete
And ev'ry minute with you in it is a treat
These moments come
And all too few
But they're enough when you have me and I have you

BOTH   *Now, lighter than a feather*
We're a happy band of laughing cavaliers.
When we are both together
We have love to guide us both throughout the years

BOB (*spoken*) Now, Tim, what else do we need?

TIM (*gleefully*) The pudding, Pa. The pudding.

BOB (*teasing*) No! Who'd have thought it? A pudding? On Christmas Day?

TIM There has to be a pudding, Pa. You said so yourself.

BOB And how very right you are, Tim! What is Christmas without? And we shall have the very best … well, the best a penny can buy.

Bob and Tim pick out a Christmas pudding. They sing to it and Bob gives the vendor a penny.

BOB *Good things come*
To those who wait

TIM *The grandest Christmas pudding ever on your plate*

BOB *As sweet as you*

TIM *And bigger too*

BOB *And we'll be dining like the Maharajahs do*
We've bought the goose
We'll feast like lords

TIM *And Mum'll make a dinner that could win awards*

BOB *But all the things*
That we could buy
They don't compare to what we have both you and I

BOTH *Now, lighter than a feather*
We're a happy band of laughing cavaliers.
When we are both together
We have love to guide us both throughout the years

As they pass the toy stall which is laden with brightly coloured toys, a number of spoilt children are telling their mother what they want. Tim and Bob stop to watch.

SPOILT CHILD#1 *I want a train*
I want a boat

SPOILT CHILD#2 *I want a dolly with a purple velvet coat*

SPOILT CHILD#1 *That soldier there*
Made out of wood

PARENT *Well, good things only come to children if they're good*

Bob and Tim pass the drinks cart. A woman is trying to drag her drunken husband from its clutches.

DRUNK *I want a drink*

WIFE *Well times are tough*

DRUNK *I think I'll have a gin*

WIFE *I think you've had enough*

TIM *No gifts galore*
Or presents new
I have the gift of love to share from me to you

BOTH *Now, lighter than a feather*
We're a happy band of laughing cavaliers.
When we are both together
We have love to guide us both throughout the years

ALL *Good things come*
To those who wait
No matter who from me and you to heads of state
But all I know
This much is true
That all the good things now are bundled up in you
When you are near
My world's complete
And ev'ry minute with you in it is a treat
These moments come
And all too few
But they're enough when you have me and I have you

VENDORS *We have enough when you have me and I have you*

BOB *They're world enough when you have me and I have you*

As the crowds disperse, Scrooge crosses towards his front door, followed by two gentlemen. One is Dickens in overcoat and top hat and the other a very portly fellow with a long muffler.

DICKENS	Ah, Mr Scrooge, I believe
SCROOGE	You may believe what you wish to believe.
DICKENS	Have I the pleasure of addressing Mr Scrooge?
SCROOGE	Pleasure? I can assure you, sir, it is not my pleasure and I'm sure it will not be yours.
GENTLEMAN#2	Nonsense, Mr Scrooge, we always gain pleasure from the generosity of our friends.
SCROOGE	Generosity? What is this?
GENTLEMAN#2	We represent the Benevolent Society for the Prevention of Poverty, sir!
SCROOGE	Bah!
DICKENS	At this festive season of the year, Mr Scrooge, it is more than usually desirable that we should make some small provision for the poor and destitute who suffer greatly at the present time.
GENTLEMAN#2	Many thousands are in want of common necessaries; hundreds of thousands are in want of common comforts, sir.
SCROOGE	Are there no prisons?
GENTLEMAN#2	Plenty of prisons, sir.
SCROOGE	And the Union workhouses? Are they still in operation?
GENTLEMAN#2	They are, sir. Still, I wish I could say they were not.
SCROOGE	Oh, I was afraid, from what you said at first, that something had occurred to stop them in their useful course.
GENTLEMAN#2	Excuse me?
SCROOGE	You're excused!

DICKENS	Er … A few of us are endeavouring to raise a fund to buy the poor some meat and drink, and means of warmth. We choose this time, because it is a time, of all others, when want is keenly felt and abundance rejoices.
GENTLEMAN#2	What can we put you down for?
SCROOGE	Nothing!
GENTLEMAN#2	You wish to be anonymous?
SCROOGE	I wish to be left alone.
GENTLEMAN #2	We were hoping you would give a little something, sir, to help your fellow man …
SCROOGE	Give something? I don't make merry myself at Christmas and I can't afford to make idle people merry. I help to support the establishments I have mentioned. They cost enough. And those who are badly off must go there.
DICKENS	The poorhouse, sir? Many can't go there. And many would rather die.
SCROOGE	If they would rather die, they had better do it and decrease the surplus population.
GENTLEMAN#2	Sir, we are here on Earth to do good for others.
SCROOGE	Then what are the others here for? Not a penny!
DICKENS	(*almost pleading*) Mr Scrooge, are you sure you won't reconsider?
SCROOGE	I know my mind, Gentlemen, and I know my business. So let me go about mine, and I will leave you to yours. Good evening!

The gentlemen shake their heads and exit.

SCROOGE	Parasites and leeches! What is it about Christmas that brings them oozing from every nook and cranny. The streets are infested with 'em! Makes my skin crawl.

On the whisper of the wind, Marley's voice is heard.

MARLEY	Scroooooooooge!

MUSIC CUE 4A

SCROOGE   *(turning suddenly)* What was that?

The knocker of the great front door to his chambers transforms into the face of Marley bathed in a dismal light. It stares at Scrooge, sorrowfully. Scrooge cautiously moves towards it.

MARLEY   Scroooooooooge!

As the face fades Scrooge reaches out to touch it

SCROOGE   Marley? Jacob Marley?

The door opens suddenly and very loudly and a walking bundle of sheets appears. Scrooge jumps back having seen one spectre, there is another on its way. The bundle unravels to reveal Mrs Dilber followed by Mrs Filch

MRS DILBER   Laundry day, Mr Scrooge!

MRS FILCH   'Ere, you look as if you've seen a ghost.

SCROOGE   *(still dazed)* Marley …

MRS DILBER   Mr Marley? He's been dead these past seven Christmases, Mr Scrooge. Bless me, whatever brought that into your head?

SCROOGE   I thought I saw … I mean to say… never mind.

MRS FILCH   Seven years dead this very night. Terrible it was. Dead as a doornail, whatever that's supposed to mean. Nightmarish! Sitting in his chair, face all wracked with hideous pain and horrifying anguish. (*She mimes the scene*) I hope he went peacefully.

MRS DILBER   Are you sure you're all right, Mr Scrooge?

SCROOGE   The wind, nothing more.

MRS FILCH   Oh, I get that something chronic.

SCROOGE   Is there a reason you're hanging around my door?

MRS FILCH   It's traditional to tip your charwoman at Christmas, Mr Scrooge.

SCROOGE   I'll give you a tip. Use less starch.

MRS FILCH   Well, thank you for nothing.

MRS DILBER   We'll be back with clean sheets in the morning, Mr Scrooge.
              Maybe I'll plate you up a little something for Christmas.

SCROOGE   I don't need your charity.

MRS DILBER   Right you are! Please yourself. I daresay it'll be eaten
              whatever comes about.

SCROOGE   Just see you get those sheets back first thing.

Scrooge slams the door on them.

MRS DILBER   Did you see the miserable old penny pincher? Eyes like
              dinner plates.

MRS FILCH   If you ask me, he's going the same way old Marley did.

MRS DILBER   White as a sheet, he was.

MRS FILCH   Whiter than any sheet I've washed.

MRS DILBER   That's not difficult. You're frugal with the soap at the best of
              times.

MRS FILCH   'Ere, just you say that to my face.

MRS DILBER   (*squaring up to her*) I said, you're frugal with the soap.

MRS FILCH   (*backing down*) Just checking. So what you up to for Christmas?

MRS DILBER   Well, me husband's on the lookout for a nice big bird.
              (*Looking at Mrs Filch, knowingly*) Let's hope he doesn't find
              one or I'll be out on my ear.

*They cackle raucously as they make their way off. Fade out as the clock on the moon
shows the hour of ten and we hear distant chimes.*

MUSIC CUE 4B

*Scrooge, robed for bed, makes his way across the upper gantry by candlelight and down
the stairs to his bed chamber. A large four-poster bed with curtains, a servants bell on
the wall, an armchair, a fireplace and a full length mirror.*

SCROOGE   (*a little shaken*) Light headedness, that's all. All this poppycock
              about Christmas always gives me distemper. Phantoms on

doorknockers – bah, fantasies of the mind! Absolute balder-
dash! Must be a head cold, nothing more! A little upset and
I'm persecuted by goblins all of my own making. Something
to line the stomach will keep these foolish ideas at bay.

*Scrooge stokes the fire, takes a small pot from the side and sits down before the fire to take
his gruel. Scrooge takes a mouthful of gruel. A ghostly whisper is heard like the wind.*

MARLEY   Ebenezer Scrooge!

*Scrooge shivers and darts his eyes about the room. He rises to get his dressing gown
from the back of the door. It rises slowly and moves across the room to the bedstead. He
rubs his eyes and looks again.*

SCROOGE   Humbug!

*Scrooge paces the room, feeling unsettled. After several turns, and more than a few
nervous glances at the door, he looks into the dressing gown. Slowly he slides one arm
through and is frightened by his hand appearing through the sleeve.*

SCROOGE   Utter nonsense.

MUSIC CUE 4B FADES

*He sits down fastening his dressing gown. As he sits, a disused bell, that hangs in the
room begins to swing. It swings so softly at the outset that it scarcely makes a sound;
but soon it rings out loudly, and for the next twenty seconds, so does every bell in the
house. All at once, the bells cease. Silence. Scrooge looks about him. Suddenly and
sharply, the sound of a downstairs door flying open with a deafening booming sound
followed by an echoing clanking noise comes from deep down below, as if some person
were dragging a heavy chain A low groan getting louder is heard.*

SCROOGE   *(talking to himself)* It's humbug still! I won't believe it.

*The groan becomes a wail as JACOB MARLEY'S GHOST rises through the floor,
and passes into the room before Scrooge's very eyes. Upon its coming in, the dying flame
leaps up in the fire-place. The ghost rises in the air, his hair a wild shock, in his usual
waistcoat, tights, and boots. A wrapper, a folded kerchief is bound about Marley's head
and chin. A long chain is clasped about his middle, wound about him like a tail; and
made of cash-boxes, keys, padlocks, ledgers, deeds, and heavy purses wrought in steel.
They reach like garlands to the flies and wings like a vast spider web and suspend him
mid-air like a marionette. The chains creak.*

SCROOGE	How now! What do you want with me?
MARLEY	Much!
SCROOGE	Who are you?
MARLEY	Ask me who I was.
SCROOGE	Who were you then?
MARLEY	In life I was your partner, Jacob Marley.

Marley sits down on the canopy of the four-poster bed. Scrooge stares at the ghost's fixed, glazed eyes as it sits perfectly motionless.

SCROOGE	Marley?
MARLEY	You don't believe in me.
SCROOGE	I don't.
MARLEY	You doubt your senses?
SCROOGE	Never!
MARLEY	Then why doubt them now?
SCROOGE	You're indigestion. That's what you are. You're probably a bit of undigested beef. There's more of gravy than of grave about you.

At this, the spirit raises a frightful cry, and shakes its chain with such a dismal and appalling noise, that Scrooge holds on tight to his chair, to save himself from falling in a swoon.

SCROOGE	Mercy! Dreadful apparition, why do you trouble me?
MARLEY	Man of the worldly mind! Do you believe in me or not?
SCROOGE	I do. I must. But why are spirits walking the earth, and why do they come to me?

MUSIC CUE 5. LINK BY LINK (MARLEY'S SONG)

Marley wails bloodcurdlingly as he rises in the air. Scrooge cowers behind his chair.

MARLEY **Sorrow bitter sorrow**
For tomorrow and tomorrow

I am damned to walk abroad with humankind
Witness what I cannot share
Throughout my life I didn't care
So now it's scored upon my tortured mind
What I never ever knew before
Is how I should reach out and help the needy and the poor
All men should deride me
Happiness denied me
Pity! Woe betide me!
It's time to settle up that dreadful score!

SCROOGE   You are bound, Jacob?

MARLEY   I wear the chain I forged in life. Each and every link upon this eternal chain I made of my own free will. And, if I could, I would break every single one but, they are my burden. My penance. Every time I turned my back on those who needed my help, I made another link. Heed me, Scrooge! Turn your back on life at your peril!

Listen to me, silent, spellbound
Lest ye carry onward hell bound
Hear me now, my time is almost gone
Look to me, a man transparent
You can see that it's apparent
That this chain goes on and on and on
Oh, the clanking
Oh, the weight
It's time to change your ways or this will be your fate

The tortured souls enter from many different places in the room. Out of cupboards, through the fireplace, over the canopy on the bed and through its curtains. Scrooge spins at all the apparitions from many different eras, but all wearing the same chains, lock boxes, and keys.

Link by link
We forge it
Yard by Yard, it's true
Misery
We gorge it
This bitter pill will soon be yours to chew

SOULS	*Oo-oo-oo-oo-oo-oo-oo-oo-oooh!*

MARLEY   *Link by link*
It's stronger
Yard by yard, we know
Yours is getting longer
'Twas long as this some seven years ago

SOULS   *O-o-oh! O-o-oh!*

MARLEY   *(gesturing toward a particularly dreadful ghoul)*
Jeremiah, tortured creature
You can tell by every feature
He's been hounded by the very hordes of hell
All his days he was a miser
Since he met the Equaliser
Now he's found he's lost his interest as well
All the pennies
All his cash
Are naught to him now he is dust to dust and ash to ash.

Edgar lost
His senses
And now
Here's the crux
Claimed on his
Expenses
For a floating home just built for ducks

SOULS   *Have to love those lucky little ducks!*

MARLEY   *For a man*
With learning
You'd think
He would know
All that he
Was earning
Was a first class ticket to the world below

SOULS   *O-o-oh! O-o-oh!*
See us once bankers dealing equity and trust
What are we since our life insurances went bust

> *All our capital and all our gains*
> *We've cashed them in for dirty rotten chains*

MARLEY *Overflowing purses*

SOULS *No use to us now*
Riding in our hearses

MARLEY *Death foreclosed on all concerns and how!*

SOUL #1 I used to be filthy stinking rich and now look at me.

SOUL #2 Well, two out of three isn't bad.

Instrumental and dance of the souls.

MARLEY Not a soul among us saw the suffering around us. Blind we were to the needs of others.

SOULS Blind!

MARLEY Now we are doomed to walk the Earth and witness what we cannot change however hard we would try.

SOULS Doomed!

MARLEY Not one ounce of pity had I in my heart.

SOULS Pity!

MARLEY Oh! Such a man was I, Ebenezer! Such was I!

SCROOGE But you were always a good man of business, Jacob.

MARLEY Business! Mankind was my business. The welfare of all was my business. Charity, mercy, care were all my business. (*wailing*) Hear me!

SCROOGE I have little choice.

MARLEY I am here this night to warn you. You have yet a chance to escape my fate.

SCROOGE You were always a good friend to me.

MARLEY You will be haunted by three spirits.

SCROOGE And that's good, is it?

MARLEY	Expect the first when the clock strikes one. The second on the stroke of two and the third at three …
	Time is swift, the seconds fleeting
	Whirring onward, no retreating
	Minutes fly without a passing glance
	Anyone who's worth an ounce'll
	Heed the spirits, hear their counsel
	Just this once you've got a second chance
MARLEY & SOULS	*Link by link*
	We're fading
	Yard by yard, it's true
	Company
	Ceased trading
MARLEY	*Don't let the same thing happen now to you*
SOULS	*Oo-oo-oo-oo-oo-oo-oo-oo-oooh!*

As a round …

MARLEY	*Link by link by link by link by –*
SOULS#1	*Link by link by link by link by –*
SOULS#2	*Link by link by link by link by –*
MARLEY	*Link by link by link by link by –*
SOULS#1	*Link by link by link by link by –*
SOULS#2	*Link by link by link by link by –*

As they carry on, Marley wails over the top …

MARLEY	*Heed the spirits, Ebenezer, heed the spirits very well*
	Don't let the chains of mortal sin drag you straight to hell
SOULS#1	*Link by link by link by link by –*
SOULS#2	*Link by link by link by link by –*
MARLEY	*Link by link by link by link by –*
ALL	*Link!*

The fire flares up once more and smoke fills the air. Marley sinks into the fires of hell and his band of tortured souls are gone. Scrooge looks about him. He examines the area where Marley disappeared.

SCROOGE Hum ... (*the word freezes on his lips*)

Scrooge clambers into bed pulling the curtains shut around him. Fadeout. We hear snoring as the lights begin to come up on the bedchamber. A chime is heard signalling the quarter. Suddenly Scrooge's head pops out from between the bed curtains.

SCROOGE A quarter past.

Scrooge disappears back behind the curtains. The chime is heard again. Scrooge's head pops out from the side curtains this time.

    Half past.

Scrooge disappears behind the curtains again. Again the chime. His head is out once more.

    A quarter to it.

He is gone again behind the curtains. Chime. Suddenly the curtains are pulled apart by Scrooge.

    (*triumphantly*) The hour itself and nothing else.

He draws the curtains closed. Pause. Slowly they are drawn back of their own accord. Scrooge sits, terrified, covers drawn up round his neck. Scrooge slips tentatively from his bed. He paces the room and as he passes the mirror, it gives off an eerie glow.

MUSIC CUE 5A

(Music Cue 5 segues into Music Cue 6, so the start of Music Cue 5a should be timed by each individual production)

We hear the crackle of flames. A figure is seen indistinctly in it, a figure that is not his own. The light grows brighter and he turns to it, shading his eyes from the glare.

SCROOGE Are you the spirit whose coming was foretold to me?

PAST   I am!

SCROOGE The glare hurts my eyes. I cannot see. Douse the light.

PAST   Would you so soon put out, with worldly hands, the light I give? I would shine upon those things forgotten.

SCROOGE Please, spirit!

The light lowers and, in the mirror, we see the shimmering form of the Ghost of Christmas Past. A softly spoken older man in white with an orange and red flame-like wig.

SCROOGE   Who and what are you?

PAST   I am the Ghost of Christmas Past

SCROOGE   Long past?

PAST   No. Your past.

SCROOGE   Might I be so bold as to ask what business brings you here?

PAST   Your welfare.

SCROOGE   A night of unbroken sleep might have been more conducive to that end.

PAST   Your reclamation then.

The light becomes bright once more so that Scrooge has to shade his eyes again. When it lowers, the Ghost of Christmas Past is standing next to him. Scrooge jumps.

SCROOGE   Er ... Will you be staying long? It's just I have a very busy day tomorrow and ...

MUSIC CUE 6. SHINE A LIGHT

PAST   Take heed. Come, look to those things that are hidden in the dark corners of your mind.

Shine a light
Into the shade
Lest your distant thoughts may fade
In every corner
In every nook
There's forgotten treasures if you take a look
The loves you found
The loves you lost
When your heart had turned to frost
Remember all
Your hopes and tears

> *Growing dimmer with the passing of the years*
> *Pierce the dark, this light of mine*
> *Let the flame of memory shine*
> *Beacon flare, my beacon bright*
> *Come with me and you will see the light*

Christmas Past begins to brighten the room. The light gets brighter until it is almost blinding fading back to reveal a snowy lane where children play. The room is gone. A small solitary boy heavily wrapped in scarf stands by a tree reading a book.

SCROOGE   (*looking about him*) Good Heaven! I know this place. Look, there's Edward. Little Tom. John. All of them here. Each and every one. Here. Now.

PAST   *Shine a light*
On all things past
Memories are built to last
No more questions
No more doubt
It's the truth your heart should never be without
No more darkness
No more spite
Take my hand and see the shining of the light

SCROOGE   (*calling*) Tom! Edward!

Scrooge approaches them but none acknowledge him. Scrooge turns quizzically to Christmas Past.

PAST   These are but shadows of the things that have been. They have no consciousness of us.

SCROOGE   This is my youth, Spirit.

PAST   A thousand thoughts, Ebenezer, a thousand hopes, a thousand joys and cares long, long forgotten.

Dickens as a tall, willowy schoolmaster enters. He rings a school bell.

DICKENS   Gentlemen, the coaches are here. Homeward bound, boys. No more schooling. The bell has rung for Christmas.

SCROOGE   Why, it's old Willow! Dear Old Willow!

DICKENS   A Merry Christmas to you all. Your trunks have been taken down. Gather your belongings and off you go, boys, no reason to be dawdling when family awaits.

The boys run off variously shaking hands, shouting their greetings until the stage is empty save for the solitary boy at the tree. Dickens looks at him sadly. The boy does not look up from his book. Scrooge and Christmas Past look on.

PAST   The school is not quite deserted. A solitary child, neglected by his friends, is left there still.

Scrooge turns away. He has let slip a tear.

         Your lip is trembling. And what is that upon your cheek?

SCROOGE   (*trying to compose himself*) It is nothing. The cold air. Nothing more.

DICKENS   (*to the boy, softly*) Ebenezer, come. There is warmth within the schoolroom.

Dickens exits as the boy looks up. Scrooge watches sadly.

PAST   One solitary child.

SCROOGE   I had my books. (*in awe*) Pages filled with wonder, spirit. Ali Baba, poor as a church mouse. Sultans and princesses. Wicked genies. Parrots of green and gold. Swordfights and peacocks. All in the pages of my book.

         These were company enough for me.

PAST   What of family?

SCROOGE   Family?

The fictional figures blend into the background with the boy reaching out for them and all is grey and cold once more.

PAST   It is a time for love and a time to be within the bosom of those who love. Those who wait upon your return with tears in their eyes. Those who welcome you to their Christmas feasting. Those who make you feel you belong.

SCROOGE   (*Hard*) Belong? When did I ever belong?

PAST	There was one who loved you, Ebenezer. She who loved you dearly. Has your heart grown so cold that your memory fades so fast? Does the child stand so truly alone?
SCROOGE	(*looking at the child*) Poor Boy! I wish … but it is too late now.
PAST	What is the matter?
SCROOGE	Nothing. Nothing. There was a boy singing a Christmas carol at my door last night. I should like to have given him something, that's all.
PAST	(*smiling*) Let us see another Christmas. Look yonder.

As Christmas Past speaks, the boy walks behind the tree and his older self comes from the other side in one movement. An older boy takes the place of the younger. He holds a book which he reads. A little girl, Fan, enters. Scrooge sees her.

SCROOGE	(*whispered*) Fan
FAN	Ebenezer.

Fan steps toward Scrooge with outstretched arms as if to embrace him. Scrooge opens his arms and walks toward her. Fan moves but passes Scrooge to run to her brother, the older boy. She throws her arms about the boy's neck.

FAN	Dear, dear brother. I have come to bring you home, dear brother. (*excitedly*) To bring you home, home.
YOUNG SCROOGE	Home, little Fan?
FAN	(*Gleefully*) Yes. Home for good and all. Home for ever and ever. Father is so much kinder than he used to be and now home's like Heaven!
YOUNG SCROOGE	For you, Fan, but not for me. He does not know me nor I him.
FAN	I asked if you might come home. And he said yes, Ebenezer, yes. And he sent me in a coach to fetch you and you're to be a man!
YOUNG SCROOGE	And you are quite the little woman, Fan.

FAN   You're never to come back here. (*Dancing round him*) But first, we're to be together all the Christmas long and have the merriest time in the world.

Fan claps and laughs. Young Scrooge smiles and catches her up in his arms and swings her round.

YOUNG SCROOGE   Dear Fan! Dear, dear Fan!

Fan grabs him by the hand and laughing pulls him away. He begins to laugh and they both exit.

PAST   (*watching them exit*) Always a delicate creature, whom a breath might have withered, but she had a large heart.

SCROOGE   She had, Spirit. That she had.

PAST   She died a woman and had, I think, children.

SCROOGE   One child.

PAST   True. Your nephew.

SCROOGE   Fred. Yes.

PAST   (*after a pause*) And so the Christmases fly on the wind. A year is but a breath. One moment and we are older.

The snowy trees part to reveal the interior of the Fezziwig's Warehouse. Two clerks sit at desks scribbling. There are wooden boxes of tea and many piles of paper and ledgers. The two clerks are Young Marley and Young Ebenezer.

PAST   You know this place?

SCROOGE   Know it? I was apprenticed here.

Fezziwig enters brightly, sprightly on his feet for a hugely rotund fellow. Beaming from ear to ear and excited.

    And there's Old Fezziwig, bless my heart. Old Fezziwig, alive again!

FEZZIWIG   Yo ho there! Ebenezer! Jacob! Yo ho, my boys! No more work tonight! Christmas Eve, Jacob! Christmas, Ebenezer! Clear away, my lads, and let's have lots of room here!

Young Ebenezer and Young Jacob are up from their desks and, quick as a flash, they clear their desks and push them back.

> Let's trim up the old place! Baubles and garlands! Ribbons and bows! Up, up with them and down with work! Let's have laughter and joy and forget our cares! Make room for the dancefloor!

A number of clerks enter and trim the place and a large table of glorious fare is pulled on. Dickens enters with a fiddle and Fezziwig greets him heartily. The whole room is bathed in the warmth of a golden glow

> What is a ball without music? And we have here a musician unparalleled in his craft. Welcome, sir, welcome, grab a glass and be merry. Fiddle music is improved by drink. Ask any Irishman.

DICKENS   Is that in the listening or the playing?

FEZZIWIG   Both!

Mrs Fezziwig enters, a large jolly woman bright in huge ball gown and giggling away.

MRS FEZZIWIG Oh, my love, you've done us proud once again. Look at the spread. Such fancies! You are determined to feed me up.

MR FEZZIWIG   Of course, my dear, there'll be so much more of you to love.

Fezziwig grabs her and swings her round. She giggles infectiously.

MRS FEZZIWIG The guests, my dear, the guests!

MUSIC CUE 6A

Suddenly the room is alive with guests arriving, excitedly, laughing, chattering and giving the blessings of the season to their hosts and to each other. Mrs Fezziwig stands at the punchbowl dispensing glasses to all who come near. The room is a fairy kingdom of twinkling lights and decoration.

EBENEZER   Old Fezziwig never lets us down.

MAN1   There is nothing better in all London Town on a Christmas Eve than the Fezziwig's Annual Christmas Ball.

MAN2   I wouldn't miss it for the world!

EBENEZER	I can't think of a man so generous
MAN2	Or as hearty, bless his soul!
MAN1	So what are we waiting for? The punchbowl is ready and we have a night of merrymaking ahead of us!

Scrooge and Christmas Past have heard this exchange from their standpoint.

PAST	A small matter to make these silly folks so full of gratitude.
SCROOGE	Small?
PAST	He spends but a few pounds of your mortal money: three or four perhaps. Is that so much that he deserves this praise?
SCROOGE	It isn't the money.
PAST	(*astonished*) Not the money?
SCROOGE	He has the power to make us happy or unhappy; to make our service light or burdensome; a pleasure or a toil. The happiness he gave us was quite as great as if it cost a fortune

MUSIC CUE 6A FADES ABRUPTLY

Past watches Scrooge as something occurs to the man.

PAST	What troubles you?
SCROOGE	Nothing particular.
PAST	Something I think.
SCROOGE	No. No. I should like to be able to say a word or two to Bob Cratchit just now, that's all.

Fezziwig steps forward and quietens the crowds.

FEZZIWIG	Strike up the music. A dance, my dears, a dance. A penny for every boy and girl who steps upon this floor and joins our merry band. I shall be the first. My darling Mrs Fezziwig, will you do me the honour?
MRS FEZZIWIG	(*skipping forward joyously*) Oh, my dear, why shouldn't we? It is Christmas after all.

Music Cue 7. The Pride of the Ball – Mr and Mrs Fezziwig and Cast

Let's show these fine young things how to do it.

During the dance, Scrooge joins the festivities, running under the arms of the dancers and skipping between them

FEZZIWIG	*When I was young and much more elastical*
	I could trip the light quite fantastical
	I could do things that girls found gymnastical
	I was the pride of the ball
MRS FEZZIWIG	*When we were wed I was quite a bit shyer*
	Though I was consumed by a flaming desire
	He wasn't much good
FEZZIWIG	*But I was a tryer*
BOTH	*Which made us the pride of the ball*
	Take the floor
	And spin like a whirligig
	Hold your hat, your girly, your periwig
	This is the season for love and romance
	So take up your partner and teach them this dance
	Round the room
	The feeling is luvverly
	Dance to the strains of Roger De Coverley
	All that remains is a kiss on the cheek
	And we will be merry for all of the week
FEZZIWIG	*We could dance a polka that's charming*
MRS FEZZIWIG	*Though the guests would find it alarming*
	For I need to diet
MR FEZZIWIG	*And I need embalming*
BOTH	*But we are the pride of the ball*
FEZZIWIG	*When we danced a jig down in Chippenham*
	Stripping the willow was sure to be grippin' 'em
MRS FEZZIWIG	*I bought new knickers*

MR FEZZIWIG	*And she got a rip in 'em*
BOTH	*We were the pride of the ball*
ALL	*Take the floor* *And spin like a whirligig* *Hold your hat, your girly, your periwig* *This is the season for love and romance* *So take up your partner and teach them this dance* *Round the room* *The feeling is luvverly* *Dance to the strains of Roger De Coverley* *All that remains is a kiss on the cheek* *And we will be merry for all of the week*
FEZZIWIG	*Christmastime should make us all merry* *Still I have found I'm round as a berry* *For I like the dancing*
MRS FEZZIWIG	*And I like the sherry*
FEZZIWIG	*Which isn't surprising at all*
ALL	*Can you find a couple that's jollier* *Out of the books of Voltaire or Molière?*
FEZZIWIG	*I'm built like a bauble*
MRS FEZZIWIG	*I'm built like a collier*
ALL	*They are the pride of the ball* *It can't be denied*
FEZZIWIG	*Though they often have tried*
ALL	*They've always been pride of the ball*

Scrooge, now out of breath and happy, and The Ghost of Christmas Past observe the little ensemble of Young Ebenezer, Young Jacob Marley and their friends. Belle, as bright as her pay will allow, smiling and beautiful in her own way, emerges from the crowd.

MUSIC CUE 7A

MAN1	Look isn't that Old Fezziwig's little shopgirl?
EBENEZER	Who?

MAN2	Oh, come, come, Ebenezer, you haven't looked at anyone else all night.
SCROOGE	(*quietly, dreamlike*) Belle.
MAN1	I think the boy is in love, gentlemen.

They laugh.

MARLEY	Nonsense! Love? What is love but an idea thought up by poets.
MAN1	Jacob Marley, you're an old stick in the mud. Where's your heart?
MARLEY	I have no time for such trivial matters. And neither has Ebenezer. We'll soon have saved enough money to start up on our own.
MAN2	Your own business?
MARLEY	And why not? There is a whole world out there and we will make the most of the opportunities it brings.

Belle nears the group.

MAN1	Well, here's *your* opportunity, Ebenezer. Take it while you may.

They push him forward. Young Ebenezer stands in front of Belle stunned by her presence. She looks at him obviously waiting to be asked to dance. Scrooge urges him onward. There is a silence until all the men burst out laughing at the sheer terror in Ebenezer's eyes. Belle looks at them and flushes with embarrassment, skitters away. Fezziwig comes forward.

MUSIC CUE 7A FADES AWAY

FEZZIWIG	Well, let's not waste a moment, gentlemen. There are many flowers in this hall tonight, all of whom are waiting for their moment in the sun. Christmas is a time for love and Mrs Fezziwig and myself should like to share it with you, so now is the time gentlemen, take your loved one by the hand and lead her to the floor.

Fezziwig leads Mrs Fezziwig to the floor and starts to waltz. Couple by couple the room is filled with dancers, except for the embarrassed Young Ebenezer and Young Marley, who looks disdainfully at the display. Belle stands on her own, in her own little world.

MUSIC 8. HEART OF GOLD – BELLE

BELLE

Please, oh, please don't keep me waiting
Endless days anticipating
Dancing through the dark, please tell me
Where, where can I find
A heart gentle and kind?
Tell me where, where is the man for me?
Tell me that he's fair
Just tell me that he's good
As I dreamed he'd always be
I don't wish for a lord
I don't wish for a prince
Who will be handsome, brave and bold
Send me someone
Just that someone
Like the fairy tales I'm often told
Give me someone with a heart of gold
So play, music play on
Till the last dancer has gone
And as the stars twinkle and fade from our view
Hold fast to your dream
Though seldom it may seem
Our wishes can come true
There must, must come a time
When that loved one is mine
Who will protect me from the cold
We'll want nothing
Simply nothing
There's no treasure that a girl will ever hold
That's precious as a heart of gold

The Fezziwigs have stopped dancing as they have run out of breath and Mrs Fezziwig points out the two 'lovebirds'. Fezziwig laughs and approaches Young Ebenezer.

FEZZIWIG   Well, my boy, isn't there someone you would like to ask to dance?

EBENEZER   Dance? I'm not ... I can't ...

FEZZIWIG   (*leading him across to where Belle stands*) Of course you can. You have made no secret of it this night. There is one that would welcome your charm.

Ebenezer stands before Belle. Belle casts her eyes down. Young Ebenezer looks back to Fezziwig. Fezziwig smiles reassuringly. Mrs Fezziwig comes to his side smiling. Ebenezer looks to Belle.

SCROOGE   (*from his standpoint*) Ask, go on, ask ...

EBENEZER   May I ... (*he clears his throat*) I was wondering if I might ... Would you like ...

BELLE   (*gazing up at him and smiling, putting him out of his misery*) I would.

Ebenezer puts out his hand and Belle takes it and tentatively they start to dance. Soon the music has swept them away. The dance goes on with Young Ebenezer and Belle slowly falling in love in the space of this one dance. Marley steps forward.

MARLEY   Ebenezer, I would speak to you ...

EBENEZER   (*to Belle*) I need to ... I should ...

BELLE   Of course. I understand.

EBENEZER   Thank you ...

BELLE   Belle.

EBENEZER   Belle.

Ebenezer kisses her hand.

MARLEY   Ebenezer ...

Ebenezer bows quickly and is gone into the crowd with Marley. Belle smiles after them. The dance carries on but with the dancers fading away into the night, leaving Belle alone on the stage with The Ghost of Christmas Past and Scrooge looking on.

BELLE   **Life will go on
The dancers have gone**

> *Swirling through time till they pale in the light*
> *One mem'ry alone*
> *I'll call my own of the love I found this night*
> *Lost in my fate*
> *The story will wait*
> *Wait for an ending to unfold*
> *Never ending*
> *Happy ending*
> *Send an ending like the fairytales of old*
> *And it finish with a heart of ...*
> *Time to stop this masquerading*
> *Who cares that the dream is fading?*
> *I have found that precious heart of gold*

Belle slowly exits.

SCROOGE	(*in a trance*) Belle.
PAST	There was once love in your heart, Ebenezer.
SCROOGE	(*snapping out of it*) Bah, a childish affectation that is all. What is love but an idea thought up by poets.
PAST	These are not your words but another's. Once your mind was not clouded by earthly matters.
SCROOGE	Earthly matters? What else is there but earthly matters?
PAST	Much, Ebenezer, much. Quick, my time is short. The years flow swiftly onwards.

A cold winter's day. Young Marley and Ebenezer walk across the stage in front of them both.

MARLEY	I have reviewed our finances, Ebenezer, we have enough to put a down payment on the premises we looked at. It is time we grew our enterprise.
EBENEZER	A larger establishment, Marley?
MARLEY	Of course, business is brisk. We are going to be rich men.

Belle enters in a mourning dress. She stops.

BELLE	Ebenezer.

Ebenezer turns to see her. Marley walks away.

> I would speak with you.

EBENEZER I have business to attend to, Belle. Might we not talk of this later?

BELLE The time has come. I cannot wait any longer.

The conversation carries on in mime show while Scrooge and Past speak together.

SCROOGE (*to Past, realising*) Please, spirit, I cannot ... not this ...

MUSIC CUE 8A

(Music Cue 8a segues into Music Cue 9, so the start of Music Cue 8a should be timed by each individual production)

PAST It is a shadow of your own making, Ebenezer. You cannot erase the past. Greed has changed you, you wear the mask of profit and gain.

EBENEZER Why do you say this now? I have not changed!

BELLE Another has taken my place, Ebenezer, a love stronger than you have shown me in a long time. The love of money.

EBENEZER I do all for us, Belle. The world is a heartless place and there is nothing that hits hard as poverty.

BELLE You fear the world too much.

EBENEZER I know the world.

BELLE And I know your heart. It has changed. Once you told me that you admired Mr Fezziwig for his generosity and kindness and that you would be like him. Do your clerks think the same of you?

EBENEZER Fezziwig was a fool.

SCROOGE (*suddenly*) He was twice the man you are!

EBENEZER I am not changed toward you, am I?

BELLE You think not? I have watched all your ideals fall away one by one. We were once content to be poor. We had one another. You were a different man then.

EBENEZER	I was a boy.
BELLE	My heart has not changed, Ebenezer, but yours has grown cold. This ring ... (*She takes it from her finger*) You gave me this when you were the Ebenezer I knew. That man has long since gone. Tell me; two years ago you asked this poor girl to marry you, would you do so now? A girl without a penny to her name from a poor family? I think not.
EBENEZER	Belle ...
BELLE	I loved you, Ebenezer, but love is not enough. It cannot be measured in shillings, pounds and pence. Therefore, (*placing the ring in his hand*) I release you from your promise.
SCROOGE	No, spirit, no!
EBENEZER	Have I ever sought release?
BELLE	In words, no, but in everything else. You are free now. Free to do whatever you wish!
SCROOGE	(*To Ebenezer*) Stop her man! She is leaving you! Damn you! Look at her! Look what you lose!
BELLE	I will soon become but an unprofitable dream you once had and time will dull all.
SCROOGE	No, no, no!
BELLE	May you be happy in the life you have chosen.
SCROOGE	(*As Belle walks away, to Ebenezer*) Go after her, you fool! Don't let her slip through your fingers! She cannot ... she cannot ... Oh, you damn fool ...

Scrooge breaks down as Belle exits. Ebenezer stands alone. Ebenezer looks down at the ring in his hand.

MUSIC CUE 9. REMEMBER – SCROOGE & YOUNG EBENEZER

SCROOGE	*Remember* *When summer was new* *Remember* *A sky built of blue*

Remember
The places we knew in our youth
Remember
The love in her eyes
Remember
When she was the prize
Remember
There was no disguising the truth
She was my all, my everything
Nature used all of her art
She took away what the clouds would bring
She was the sun in my heart
Seasons would fly like the birds on wing
She made the golden leaves gleam
She was my all, my everything
She made the world like a dream

EBENEZER   Forget her
I'll learn to forget
Forget her
The sun will still set
Forget her
It's better to let her just go
Forget her
Let time take its toll
Forget her
My heart and my soul
Forget her
Though she made me whole, this I know
She was my all, my everything
Nature used all of her art
She took away what the clouds would bring
She was the sun in my heart
Seasons would fly like the birds on wing
She made the golden leaves gleam
She was my all, my everything
She made the world like a dream

Both Scrooge and Young Ebenezer sing in canon their own verses up until …

BOTH	*She was my all, my everything* *Nature used all of her art* *She took away what the clouds would bring* *She was the sun in my heart*
SCROOGE	*Winter was cold when she walked away* *Icy the wind to be sure* *Bitter the cold growing every day* *Frost pierced my love to the core*
EBENEZER	*Forget her* *Let time take its toll*

Young Ebenezer slowly exits.

SCROOGE	**Remember** **Remember** *(almost a sob)* **Remember**
SCROOGE	Enough, Spirit, why do you torment me so?
PAST	I, torment you?
SCROOGE	Remove me from this place

The light begins to fade as Past speaks the following line. Past is fading.

PAST	I told you these were shadows of the things that have been. They are what they are, do not blame me.
SCROOGE	Remove me. I cannot bear it.

The bedchamber appears and Scrooge sits wearily on the bed.

> I cannot bear it.

He drops his head into his hands and the lights fade. The ever present moon shines down and slowly upon its face the clock appears. It reads just off one o'clock. Scrooge's room is dark and he lies asleep. He awakes with a start. Sitting up, he lights his candle. He darts his eyes about the room. Just as he has assured himself nothing will happen, the clock strikes two.

SCROOGE   *(after each chime)* One … Two … There, nothing. Bah.

He blows out his candle and settles to sleep.

MUSIC CUE 9A
*(Music Cue 9a segues into Music Cue 10, so the start of Music Cue 9a
should be timed by each individual production)*

*Suddenly a bright light and the sound of booming laughter fills the room and Scrooge
sits bolt upright. He shades his eyes.*

PRESENT   Scrooge!

SCROOGE   *(slamming his pillow over his head to blot it all out)* I'm asleep.

PRESENT   Scrooge!

SCROOGE   You'll wake the dead.

PRESENT   Scrooge!

*Throughout this the Spirit of Christmas Present has been trucked on atop a glorious
array of Christmas fare. Bright gleaming berries glisten, crisp leaves of holly, mistletoe
and ivy reflect like little mirrors and a mighty fire roars in the fireplace. Turkeys, geese,
game, poultry, brawn, great joints of meat, suckling-pigs, long wreaths of sausages, mince
pies, plum puddings, barrels of oysters, red-hot chestnuts, cherry cheeked apples, juicy
oranges, luscious pears, immense twelfth cakes and seething bowls of punch that make
the room dim with their delicious steam form a throne where there sits a jolly giant
clothed in one simple deep green robe bordered with white fur. Bare chested and
barefooted but with a holly wreath upon its head from which hangs sparkling icicles.
Round about its vast midriff is a belt.*

PRESENT   Come, little man, come and know me better.

Scrooge climbs from his bed tentatively.

            Closer so that I may see the measure of the man.

*Scrooge stands cowering a little and the Ghost of Christmas Present lets out a huge
roar of laughter.*

            Well, well, so much trouble for one so small. A sorrier
            looking specimen I never did see!

SCROOGE   Who … who are you?

PRESENT   I am the Ghost of Christmas Present. Look upon me.

Scrooge, who has been averting his eyes thus far, looks at him.

            You have never seen the like of me before!

SCROOGE	Never.
PRESENT	I see we have much work to do. You do not even recognise this Christmas spirit.
SCROOGE	I think I should have remembered if I'd seen it before. It's not a thing one would forget.
PRESENT	And yet my brothers have visited this world many, many times.
SCROOGE	Brothers?
PRESENT	Yes, one for every year. Over eighteen hundred of them.
SCROOGE	That is a monstrous family to provide for.
PRESENT	And yet we rejoice.
SCROOGE	Bah. More fool you.
PRESENT	Fool, am I? Ha, you know so little. All the world is celebrating, Ebenezer, and you are the only one who does not. They go about their business with joy in their souls and a smile on their lips though they have nothing but the clothes in which they stand.
SCROOGE	I have no reason to be joyous.
PRESENT	And they have?

MUSIC CUE 10. DRINK IT IN

PRESENT	A man may have nothing in this world but he can make it a paradise by the way he lives his life. You have it all before you and go about with your eyes cast to the ground. Look up, Ebenezer, look up.

Take a chance at living for the time you have is brief
Use it, it's the only life you've got
The way that you exist, my friend, it beggars all belief
Life is hard, you say, but hard compared to what?
Time rolls ever onward
Life will wend its way
What have we to live for if it isn't for today?

> *Drink it in*
> *Don't be languid, limp and listless*
> *Drink it in*
> *Take a draft of Merry Christmas*
> *Lift a glass and feel the spirit warm the cockles of the heart*
> *Ancient grudges and ill feeling; set the silly things apart*
> *For the season of goodwill and love is just about to start*
> *Drink it in! Drink it in! Drink it in!*

SCROOGE   That is all very well, Spirit, but I thought you were here to teach me something.

PRESENT   I can only teach if a pupil is ready to learn. Are *you* ready, Ebenezer Scrooge?

SCROOGE   I am as ready as I will ever be. Lead me where you will.

PRESENT   Then rise up, little man, rise up.

Scrooge rises into the air followed by Christmas Present during the next verse. The room swirls away bringing Scrooge and the spirit above London. Below them we see the bustle of the street we saw at the top of Act one. The last hours of Christmas Eve. The Christmas rush.

PRESENT   *Drink it in*
> *Don't be spiteful; rise above it*
> *Drink it in*
> *And I know that you will love it*
> *Though you may be old and blinkered and your mind will not allow*
> *Flying high above this planet; see the world as it is now*
> *Soften up that hardened heart and be a better man somehow*
> *Drink it in! Drink it in! Drink it in!*

PRESENT   Look, look, Ebenezer! See below you a world you have never seen before.

SCROOGE   There is *something* about it, Spirit.

PRESENT   Something you've never experienced? In all your years, little man, you have never been part of it. It's little wonder you know it not. It's called life, Ebenezer. Life!

Present spreads out his hand and stardust falls on those below. They are touched with the spirit of Christmas.

PRESENT	**Drink it in**
GROUP1	**It's a cause for celebration**
PRESENT	**Drink it in**
GROUP2	**Every sound and each sensation**
WOMAN1	**Every child is filled with wonder at the treats that lie in store**
WOMAN2	**Every stocking waits for filling hanging on the chamber door**
PRESENT	**Every Christmas thought is thrilling everybody to the core**
ALL	**Drink it in! Drink it in! Drink it in!**
SAM	Evenin' Charlie. Looking forward to a bit of a knees up tomorrow?
COSTERMONGER	What do you think? The wife's mother's coming round.
SAM	Well, it *is* a time for goodwill to all humankind.
COSTERMONGER	That's the trouble. She ain't human.
SAM	Ah well, I've been married to my girl for so many years now, I've developed an attachment for my mother in law.
COSTERMONGER	Really?
SAM	Yes, it fits over her mouth.
ALL	**Drink it in** **'Tis the season you should savour** **Drink it in** **Take a sup, enjoy the flavour**
COSTERMONGER	**Making merry though your days be full of worry, woe and strife**
WOMAN1	**Taking time to see that Christmas brings the brighter side of life**

WOMAN2   *Let the snowflakes take your troubles*

SAM   *Take my troubles? Take the wife!*

ALL   *Drink it in! Drink it in! Drink it in!*

Scrooge and the Ghost of Christmas Present have descended to the ground where the bustle has begun again. They watch as life passes with the joy of Christmas Eve. A man and a very drunk woman pass.

MAN   *Drink it in*

WOMAN   *I've been feeling fairly frisky*

MAN   *Drink it in*
            Have another tot of whiskey

WOMAN   *You're a naughty, naughty fella who would lead a girl astray*
            You might tempt me for an hour just to have your wicked way
            Just another bottle now, m'dear, and it's your lucky day

ALL   *Drink it in! Drink it in! Drink it in!*

Dance.

ALL   *Ding Dong!*
            Sing a Christmas carol
            Ding Dong!
            Sing it clear
            Ding Dong!
            Open up a barrel
            Come and raise a toast with Christmas cheer

Dance.

PRESENT   *Taste the Christmas flavour; let it season all you do*
            Sprinkle joy and laughter, come what may
            Life is more than pennies and the interest you accrue
            What is money but a thing to give away?
            Friendship makes you wealthy
            Money brings just tears
            How will you be remembered in the coming years?

ALL   *Drink it in*
            Find a different man within you

> *Drink it in*
> *And I know that you'll begin to*
> *Taste the sweetness, man, instead of just the bitter and the*
> *sour*
> *Feel the light that that now surrounds you growing brighter*
> *by the hour*
> *Being generous and hearty is completely in your power*

SCROOGE   *Drink it in! Drink it in!*

PRESENT   *Let that frown become a grin*

ALL   *Drink it in! Drink it in!*

PRESENT   *Let the better life begin*

ALL   *Drink it in! Drink it in!*

PRESENT   *Be the man you are within*

ALL   *Drink it in! Drink it in! Drink it in!*

Christmas Present has some sort of 'pyrotechnic' in his staff, which flares up at the end of the number before blackout.

END OF ACT ONE

ACT II

Music Cue 11. Entr'acte

Daylight. The bells are pealing joyously. Dickens appears on the gantry. People bustle below all in their Sunday best. Greeting one another and exchanging pleasantries. All hurrying home to enjoy their Christmas Day. Children play and dart amongst them.

DICKENS   Throughout the night, far above the rooftops of London, the spirit lead Scrooge and, as they flew on the back of the wind, Scrooge was able to observe the festivities of the people below. Everywhere they went, the spirit sprinkled joy amongst his fellow men. From the grandest of gentlemen to the lowly lamplighters: every one of them joyous in the prospects of another Christmas Day.

Music Cue 12. Reprise – Good Things Come

CAST   *Good things come*
To those who wait
No matter who from me and you to heads of state
But all I know
This much is true
That all the good things now are bundled up in you
When you are near
My world's complete
And ev'ry minute with you in it is a treat
These moments come
And all too few
But they're enough when you have me and I have you
Now, lighter than a feather
We're a happy band of laughing cavaliers
When we are both together
We have love to guide us both throughout the years

Scrooge and Christmas Present fly in and stop, watching the people pass, smiling and happy.

SCROOGE   Your presence seems to bring joy to all around, spirit.

PRESENT   Warmth can be felt by those who seek it. I give what I can. There are those who need it more at this time of the year and I have enough to share. *(Music Cue 12 has faded out)* Come, follow.

The Ghost of Christmas Present leads Scrooge towards a ramshackle building and stops at its door.

SCROOGE   Spirit, why do we stop in this part of town? I have no business here.

PRESENT   You think not?

SCROOGE   I know it. What is there for me here?

PRESENT   Look closer, little man. All will be made clear.

The house turns and we see a squalid home made merry to the best of its means. A table and chairs. Mrs Cratchit wipes her hands on her apron and lifts the lid of a large pot on the stove. Her children who have been playing some child's game stop to watch her.

PETER   Is it done, Mama?

MRS CRATCHIT   *(smiling)* Is it done? Is it done? Is that all we are to hear this Christmas day? It will be done when it's done. You don't rush a pudding.

BELINDA   We shall have the best Christmas this side of Camden.

MRS CRATCHIT   That we shall, Belinda. That we shall. What ever is keeping your precious father then? And your brother Tiny Tim…

BELINDA   What about Martha, Mama?

MRS CRATCHIT   Is this family ever to be together for Christmas? Martha wasn't this late last Christmas Day.

Martha appears at the doorway.

MARTHA   Here's Martha, mother.

CHILDREN   Here's Martha.

MRS CRATCHIT   Thank heavens for that. And just in the nick of time. Bless my heart how late you are!

Mrs Cratchit kisses her and takes her in her arms.

> Sit you down by the fire, my dear, and have a warm, Lord bless ye!

As Martha sits, the two children surround her.

PETER   There's such a goose, Martha.

BELINDA   Father says it's almost as big as me.

Peter runs to the window.

PETER   Father's coming.

BELINDA   Hide, Martha, hide.

Martha hides and Bob Cratchit enters with Tiny Tim held aloft on his shoulders. Tim carries a crutch and his legs are strengthened by leg braces.

SCROOGE   Bob Cratchit! This is his home? His family?

PRESENT   It is.

BOB   Here we go, Tim, home at last. What a morning, my love. What a beautiful morning.

Bob places Tim down upon a stool and kisses his wife and spins her round.

> Merry Christmas, my love.

MRS CRATCHIT   (*laughing*) Oh, put me down, you fool.

BOB   Better to do it now. After that Christmas Dinner, I won't be able to lift you.

Mrs Cratchit swipes at him playfully. The children run and hug at him.

> Bless you, my dears, bless you. Why, where's our Martha?

MRS CRATCHIT   (*stifling a giggle*) Not coming.

BOB   (*Heartbroken*) Not coming? Not coming upon Christmas day?

Martha runs from her hiding place and grabs him round his middle from behind. The children laugh.

MARTHA   (*laughing*) Oh, father, what an awful trick to play.

MRS CRATCHIT (*looking at Tim's hands and laughing*) Well, well, look at the state of you, Tim. To the wash house with you. I want you clean as an angel before Christmas dinner. All of you. Wash house.

Belinda and Peter help Tim off.

MRS CRATCHIT How did little Tim behave at church?

BOB As good as gold. He gets so thoughtful sitting by himself and thinks the strangest things you ever heard.

Tim is heard coughing off

He told me coming home that he hoped the people saw him in the church and remembered this Christmas Day who it was that made lame beggars walk and blind men see. And he looks so much better, don't you think my dear?

MRS CRATCHIT (*almost sadly*) Yes, dear. Yes. Yes he does.

THE CHILDREN (*running in*) All clean. All clean.

Tiny Tim hobbles behind them.

TIM Mother, can we see the goose?

MRS CRATCHIT I was saving it just for you, Tim. Here it comes.

Mrs Cratchit reaches into the stove and brings out a small sorry looking bird.

SCROOGE This is it? This is their finest goose? Why, it's hardly worth the cooking.

PRESENT Watch, little man.

BOB Here we are! The finest feast I ever did see! We can make our little Christmas as grand as any king or queen. You just have to remember what it is to be a Cratchit.

MUSIC CUE 13. DO AS THE CRATCHITS DO – THE CRATCHIT FAMILY

CRATCHIT *If you take a look in a hist'ry book, you'll find us everywhere It's common sense that the great events should have a Cratchit there*

	So when you're in a pickle, and answers are too few
	Don't make a fuss, it's clear to us
	You do as the Cratchits do
ALL	Do as the Cratchits do
	Oh, do as the Cratchits do

MRS CRATCHIT   They may not have that much to spare

ALL   Whatever they have, they always share

MRS CRATCHIT   So when your cupboard's almost bare
Just do as the Cratchits do

CRATCHIT   When wotsisname and the Vikings came to plunder the British Isles
With their terrible hordes and their great big swords and their wide bloodthirsty smiles
The people shook and trembled and said to the nasty crew
'We've got no grub so join the club
And do as the Cratchits do'

ALL   Do as the Cratchits do
Oh, do as the Cratchits do

MRS CRATCHIT   They may not have that much to spare

ALL   Whatever they have, they always share

MRS CRATCHIT   So when your cupboard's almost bare
Just do as the Cratchits do

CRATCHIT   At his summer home in the mighty Rome, proud Caesar sat and stewed
Though his troops had fought, no men were caught, and he wasn't in the mood
The British starving in the wood in wode of brightest blue
'We've not been fed', the Chieftains said
'We'll do as the Cratchits do!'

ALL   Do as the Cratchits do
Oh, do as the Cratchits do

MRS CRATCHIT   They may not have that much to spare

ALL   *Whatever they have, they always share*

MRS CRATCHIT   *So when your cupboard's almost bare*
Just do as the Cratchits do

CRATCHIT   *When the people all said, 'We want our bread', though they had none to bake*
Said the Gallic threat, Marie Antoinette,

MRS CRATCHIT   *'Just let them all eat cake'*

CRATCHIT   *Her fate was sealed for she was fairly cleanly sliced in two*
She lost her head but she should have said,

MRS CRATCHIT   *'Do as the Cratchits do!'*

ALL   *Do as the Cratchits do*
Oh, do as the Cratchits do

MRS CRATCHIT   *They may not have that much to spare*

ALL   *Whatever they have, they always share*

MRS CRATCHIT   *So when your cupboard's almost bare*
Just do as the Cratchits do

ALL   *Do as the Cratchits do*
Oh, do as the Cratchits do
Though the feast was small, we've had a ball
Doing just what us Cratchits do

The family laugh. They go to begin dinner and Bob stands at the head of the table and begins to say grace as it fades to a pool of light on Scrooge and Christmas Present.

SCROOGE   They have so little and yet they rejoice.

PRESENT   They have infinitely more than you observe, Ebenezer Scrooge. They have each other.

SCROOGE   There is something in what you say, spirit.

PRESENT   The world is full of people like these, man. It is only that you have never lifted up your eyes to see. See them now …

The light comes up on a finished dinner and Bob stands, with a glass in his hand.

BOB	(*raising a toast*) Mr Scrooge! I give you Mr Scrooge, the founder of our feast.
MRS CRATCHIT	(*irate*) The Founder of the Feast indeed! If I had him here I'd give him a piece of my mind for him to feast upon and I hope he'd have a good appetite for it.
BOB	My dear, the children. Christmas Day.
MRS CRATCHIT	It would have to be Christmas Day, I'm sure, to drink the health of such a mean old skinflint as Mr Scrooge. You know he is, Robert. Nobody knows it better than you do.
BOB	(*mildly*) My dear, Christmas Day.
MRS CRATCHIT	I'll drink his health for your sake, not for his. A Merry Christmas and a Happy New Year. He'll be very merry and very happy, I have no doubt of it.
BOB	(*toasting once more*) A Merry Christmas to us all, my dears. God bless us.
ALL	God bless us
TIM	God Bless us every one!
BOB	This has been the best Christmas ever.
MARTHA	You say that every year, father.
BOB	It gets better year by year.
MRS CRATCHIT	You say that too, my dear

She kisses his head.

BOB	My, my, look at the time. Look at the time, my dears. How quickly Christmas flies. All this merrymaking. You must all be quite tired.
PETER	Not us, father.

Belinda yawns very audibly. Peter stifles a yawn after her.

BOB	Well, well, not tired, eh? Then we can all help mother tidy away and wash the dishes. What say you?
BELINDA	I'm very tired, father.

PETER   So am I.

BOB   Very well. Then come kiss me goodnight.

Peter, Belinda and Tiny Tim all kiss one by one and hug their mother. They traipse off to bed.

BOB   Say your prayers, my dears.

Bob turns to Mrs Cratchit and they embrace. The house turns and Tim, Belinda and Peter kneel by their bed. Night has fallen and the moon is once more in the night sky.

MUSIC CUE 14. GOD BLESS – TINY TIM, THE CRATCHIT CHILDREN & THE CHILDREN OF LONDON

TIM

Guide us now, Oh, holy star
Remind us who and what we are
Blessed child that you sent our way
Who was born this joyous Christmas Day

TIM & CRATCHITS
(& FEMALE/MALE
BACKING ENSEMBLE)

You who made the blind to see
Who watches over you and me
Bless the ones that we hold so dear
Bless us now today and all the year

TIM & FEMALE
BACKING ENSEMBLE

Bless the children all alone
Bless those who are far from home
Bless them all this night, I pray
Shine your love upon us
Bless the ones who've lost their way
Find them, Lord, this Christmas Day
God, I know you hear my prayer
Shine your love upon us

Peter and Belinda climb into their beds and settle down. A spot picks out Tim.

TIM & CHILDREN
(& FEMALE/MALE
BACKING ENSEMBLE)

Lord, I know that I am small
And I may not matter over all
You, who sent your only son
Bless us all, God Bless us everyone

The spot fades on Tim as Scrooge and Christmas Present look on.

SCROOGE   (*with compassion*) Spirit, tell me, will Tiny Tim live?

As the Ghost speaks, a tight spot comes up on a crutch leaning against a stool.

PRESENT   I see a vacant seat in the poor chimney corner and a crutch without an owner, carefully preserved. If these shadows remain unaltered by the future, the child will die.

SCROOGE   No, kind spirit, no. Say he will be spared.

PRESENT   (*mimicking Scrooge*) If he is to die, let him do it and decrease the surplus population.

Scrooge hangs his head in shame.

SCROOGE   (*softly, contritely*) Spirit …

PRESENT   (*hard*) What is surplus? Will you decide what men shall live, what men shall die? It may be that, in the sight of Heaven, you are more worthless and less fit to live than millions like this poor man's child.

SCROOGE   I did not mean …

PRESENT   Your words were yours alone and you are responsible for their meaning.

MUSIC CUE 14A

Suddenly jolly music pipes up, and a golden glow of a warm drawing room pools centrally. A party gathering is seen. The couples dance into the space, laughing and whooping. It is Fred's Christmas party. He and Beth, his wife, dance as a few clap and laugh from the sides. One of the guests is Dickens himself.

PRESENT   You know this place?

SCROOGE   It is not a place I recall. But I recognise my nephew. This must be his home. And this, his wife.

WOMAN   Another splendid evening!

FRED   (*To Beth*) We do our best, don't we, my dear?

WOMAN   Will your Uncle Scrooge be joining us?

FRED   (*whooping with laughter*) Uncle Scrooge? Here? You obviously don't know my Uncle Scrooge.

DICKENS	She must be the only one. He's legendary! Rich as Croesus and not one generous bone in his body!
SCROOGE	(*To Present*) I don't think I like that man.
FRED	He said that Christmas was a humbug, as I live! He believed it too!
BETH	More shame for him, Fred!
FRED	He's a comical old fellow, that's the truth, and not so pleasant as he might be, but he is his own worst enemy so I'll have nothing to say against him.
BETH	I'm sure he's awful to his clerk, or so you always tell me so!
FRED	Good Old Bob Cratchit! He's positively frightful to him.
SCROOGE	(*To Christmas Present*) I think I look after the man handsomely.
FRED	The poor man is on a pittance, I'm sure.
BETH	And with all your Uncle's wealth!
FRED	Well, it's no use to him. He don't do any good with it.
BETH	Well, I have no patience with him.
FRED	Oh, I have! I'm sorry for him. I couldn't be angry with him if I tried. Who suffers for his ill whims? Himself always. Here, he takes it into his head to dislike us, and he won't come and dine with us. What's the consequence? He loses a glorious Christmas dinner.
DICKENS	That he does! Marvellous! Any more of that pudding?
WOMAN	I think you've had enough.
PRESENT	(*To Scrooge*) We must be on our way, little man.

MUSIC CUE 14A FADES OUT

BETH	What say you all to a game?

General affirmations all round.

SCROOGE	Oh, wait! Let us stay for the game. Just one game, spirit!

PRESENT	As you wish.
FRED	Animal, vegetable or mineral. I shall think of a thing and the rest of you must find out what. I can only answer yes or no, mind you.
WOMAN	Let me go first before someone else thinks of my question. Are you animal, vegetable or mineral?
FRED	That's not a yes or no answer.
BETH	Oh, come, Fred, don't be such a stickler.
FRED	All right. Am I animal, vegetable or mineral? Oh, definitely an animal!
DICKENS	Is it a savage animal?
FRED	Oh, definitely. Fearsomely unpleasant.
BETH	A fearsomely unpleasant animal? Let me think. What could it be?
SCROOGE	It is a cat.
PRESENT	A cat?
SCROOGE	Well, *I* think they're unpleasant.
BETH	Does it talk?
FRED	Sometimes it talks, sometimes it grunts!
BETH	Is it a parrot?
FRED	Since when did a parrot grunt?
BETH	A pig?
FRED	No! It growls too, you know.
SCROOGE	A bear! That's what it is! A bear! I'll bet my shirt on it!
DICKENS	Does it live in London?
FRED	It does indeed.
WOMAN	I'm sure I have no idea whatsoever.

Fred howls with laughter.

BETH   It's a fearsomely unpleasant creature that sometimes talks and sometimes grunts. It growls and it lives in London. Whatever could it be?

Fred giggles

WOMAN   Does it live in a zoo?

FRED   No.

BETH   Wait! I have it! I have it!

Beth starts to laugh. Fred joins in. They roar with laughter.

WOMAN   Oh, come, put us out of our misery, what is it?

BETH   I know what it is, Fred! A fearsome growling animal that lives in London.

FRED   What is it?

BETH   It's Uncle Scrooge!

FRED   It is.

All laugh heartily.

SCROOGE   I'm not sure I find that in the least bit funny.

PRESENT   Strangely accurate though.

FRED   Well, the old fellow has given us plenty of merriment, I am sure, and it would be ungrateful not to drink his health. Though he rail at Christmas for eternity, I shall never stop trying to wish him the joy of the season. Uncle Scrooge!

ALL   Uncle Scrooge!

FRED   A Merry Christmas and a Happy New Year to the old man, wherever he is!

SCROOGE   (*making his way between the guests*) Thank you, thank you! Your health, too. Thank you!

The guests disperse, laughing and chattering, and the party fades away. The Ghost of Christmas Present walks with difficulty and Scrooge catches sight of the spirit's gait. They are outside once more and the night is dark. The moon looks down.

SCROOGE   Spirit, you are weary. Rest awhile.

PRESENT	I fade. My age is almost over.
SCROOGE	Are spirits' lives so short?
PRESENT	My time on upon this globe is brief. It ends tonight.
SCROOGE	But you bring light and goodness wherever you tread. How can you leave this world?
PRESENT	I am but a brief reminder. What man decides to do with this shadow is of his choosing.

MUSIC SCENE 14B

(Music Cue 14ab segues into Music Cue 15, so the start of Music Cue 14b should be timed by each individual production)

At this moment a band of dismal, ragged, bare-footed children are herded past weary through endless walking in the snow by a rotund Beadle.

My light does not shine everywhere, Ebenezer Scrooge; there are many places where it will never be allowed in. The door is barred and bolted against it by ignorance. See. Look on.

As a child falls, the Beadle grabs it by the arm and drags it unceremoniously to its feet. The Beadle pushes it back into line with his cane.

The cruelty of this city and the world is huge. Listen! You can hear the hunger, the need, the helplessness.

SCROOGE	Have they no refuge or resource?
PRESENT	*(mimicking Scrooge)* Are there no prisons? Are there no workhouses?

Scrooge bows his head in shame.

SCROOGE	*(softly)* Spirit, you mock me. What do you expect of me?
PRESENT	I expect nothing.
SCROOGE	Please. Speak comfort. Guide me.
PRESENT	Your heart should be your guide, Scrooge. Understand that first and foremost.

The light is fading and as Christmas Present slowly moves away, he takes the light with him until Scrooge is left standing alone in the street in a single spot of eerie light.

SCROOGE   (*with growing anxiety*) Wait! Please. Your light grows dim. Don't leave me alone in this darkness. Spirit, what am I to do? (*Calling*) Spirit …

MUSIC CUE 15. AM I THAT MAN

SCROOGE   *Crowded now by shadows*
Plagued by might have been (bin)
Does it take a spectre to expect a man repent his sin?
Reality and reason
What has gone before
Do I block them from my mind or open up a brand new door?
Lord knows who is watching with that damned infernal plan
Watching, wanting, hoping, as a guardian only can,
Trusting I will ask the question; who the devil is that man?

(*spoken*) Who the devil is that man?

Am I that man
Who never sees
The wretchedness he wrought on sorry souls as these?
Am I that man
Whose heart was stone
Who'll end his life a broken man and all alone?
Am I that heartless solitary man?
Am I that man
Filled with regret
About the times he could have changed the world and, yet
What is a man
Who watches blind
The suff'ring of his fellow humankind?
Am I that devil who would call himself a man?

(*spoken*) It cannot be … Could I have been so blind? How? How can I change now? Where would I start?

Spirits of my nightmare
Spirits come and go
How can I be certain of the truth in all they show
Change is always fright'ning
More than ghosts or ghouls
Other men take heed to dreams but other men are fools
What is it that starts this fever growing in my head?
What have I been shown this night which melts this heart of lead?
Why should I rush in where all the angels always fear to tread?

(*spoken*) Why should I? Why should I?

Am I that man
With reckless ease
Who'd break the mould and change the world in times like these?
Am I that man?
This much is true
This dream is but a fantasy I'll not pursue
I'll stay exactly perfect as I am
But then a man
Who doesn't bend
Will find he's barely nothing in the end
Am I that man
Who can't be free
Shackled to this life I've made for all eternity
Tell me true am I that man I see
Damn!
Tell me how
To find
Out now the kind
Of man
I am

The clock chimes three solemnly and, after a silence …

A Christmas Carol

MUSIC SCENE 15A

... a huge black cowled figure draws itself up from a darkened corner. From what was just a pile of discarded rags, grows a spectre, horrifying and grim. It grows from the ground upwards, getting ever taller. It towers above Scrooge. Slowly it moves towards him, almost hovering, mist trailing from its tattered hem.

SCROOGE   (*trembling*) Am I in the Presence of the Ghost of Christmas Yet to Come?

It reaches out a bony hand which points to Scrooge. A breathy hiss can be heard growing louder until it fills the air with its rasping death rattle. Scrooge falls to his knees.

You are about to show me shadows of the things that have not yet happened but will happen in the time before us? Is that so, Spirit?

The black cowled figure slowly inclines its head.

Ghost of the future, I fear you more than any spectre I have seen. But fearful as I am, I know I am too old to change my ways. I cannot change, spirit. I can't.

Silence.

Will you not speak to me?

Silence and then slowly the spectre's hand points away into the distance.

(*resigned*) Lead on, then, Spirit, lead on.

Music Scene 15a stops

The Spirit slowly hovers upstage and Scrooge, looking about him warily, follows tentatively. Three gentlemen in long black coats and top hats, carrying umbrellas to ward off the weather, enter. One being Dickens.

DICKENS   Devil of a day to be out in!

BUSINESSMAN#2 Wretched weather!

DICKENS   Heard the news, gentlemen?

BUSINESSMAN#3 Of course, I've heard nothing but.

BUSINESSMAN#2 How did it happen?

DICKENS   I don't know much about it either way, I only know he's dead.

SCROOGE   (*To Future*) Spirit, what has this to do with me? What man do they talk of?

BUSINESSMAN#3   When did he die?

DICKENS   Last night, I believe.

BUSINESSMAN#3   What was the matter with him?

DICKENS   God knows.

BUSINESSMAN#2   I thought he'd never die.

BUSINESSMAN#3   What has he done with all his money?

BUSINESSMAN#2   All I know is he hasn't left it to me. Had it stuffed in his coffin with him, I shouldn't wonder.

The three laugh.

SCROOGE   I know these men. What sort of man is this; that no one has a good word to say about him at his death?

DICKENS   Is anyone going to the funeral?

BUSINESSMAN#3   Will there be food?

DICKENS   I doubt it. Since when did the old man do anything to benefit his fellow man?

BUSINESSMAN#3   Well, I must be fed or I go nowhere.

BUSINESSMAN#2   I may show my face. If only to give my new black gloves an outing.

They laugh again and make their way off.

SCROOGE   Whose funeral were they talking about? No grief, no care. The man must have been a monster. Why do you show me these things, spirit?

Mrs Dilber and Mrs Filch enter with bundles.

MRS DILBER   Filthy night!

MRS FILCH	Well, all this bother will be worth it if it gives us a few bob for Christmas. About time the old miser gave us our dues.
MRS DILBER	Shame he had to go belly up before we benefitted by him.
MRS FILCH	It ain't a shame, and you know it. The bloke was a right bad 'un.
SCROOGE	I know these women. Mrs Dilber and Mrs Filch. They're in my employ. What brings them to a place such as this?

Old Joe enters pushing a cart of various detritus and stolen goods.

OLD JOE	Well met, ladies and in such weather.
MRS DILBER	Oh, get a move on, Joe, we ain't got all night.
OLD JOE	There's always time for niceties, Mrs Dilber. There's always a place for gentility.
MRS DILBER	And there's always a place for the toe of me boot. Now let's get this done.
OLD JOE	Have it your way.
MRS FILCH	We will.
OLD JOE	What have you got for Old Joe then? Pretty trinkets, my lovelies? Bit of lace? Any silver? Why don't we start with a little bit of gin to warm your bones this cold night, eh?
MRS DILBER	You won't wheedle your way round us that way, Joe. We know the going price.
OLD JOE	I know you do, Mrs Dilber. That I do. (*Grabbing her cheek*) You'll make a fortune one of these days. You've got a good eye for the fancy stuff. Top notch, I'll be betting.
MRS DILBER	Nothing but the best, Joe.
OLD JOE	Well, I ain't gonna know what I'm willing to part with unless I see the goods.

Mrs Filch drops her bundle on the floor before Old Joe.

MRS FILCH	Got a fine haul from the old skinflint. Sitting on a pot of gold, he was. Deserves all he got.

OLD JOE   (*tongue-in-cheek*) Speaking ill of the dead, Mrs Filch? Shame on you.

MRS FILCH   I ain't saying nothing that I didn't say when he was alive. Not a soul had a good word about him then. What's the difference now?

OLD JOE   (*still teasing, with hand on heart and shaking his head*) Oh, and him all alone in the world. What a wicked, wicked thing to say.

MRS DILBER   Pushed everyone from him, that he did. There won't be any love lost. Gasping his last with not a one to care whether he lived or died.

MRS FILCH   I ain't gonna weep now. I wept enough when the old screw was alive. He got what was coming to him.

OLD JOE   Ladies, ladies, let us have some decorum.

MUSIC CUE 16. JUST DESSERTS – OLD JOE, MRS DILBER & MRS FILCH

OLD JOE   *We're gathered here together for the passing of a bloke*
What's given us the greatest gift around
We're all set to make a killing

MRS FILCH   *I owed him half a shilling*

MRS DILBER   *He won't need it when he's six feet underground*

OLD JOE   *Now the Bard wrote to the letter*
And I couldn't put it better
Neither borrower nor lender ever be
But I know when all is panned out
We might need a little handout
And that handout's just been handed straight to me

MRS FILCH   *Poor old fella*
Gone to the dogs

MRS DILBER   *Debts are cancelled now the miser's gone and popped his clogs*

ALL   *Just Desserts, just desserts*
We've hit the skinflint where it really hurts

Now he's dead, each man alive'll
Know the Devil's got a rival
Anyway
It's fair to say
It's just desserts

OLD JOE   So what've you got for me, Mrs Filch?

MRS FILCH   I got a couple of nice shirts. Two silver teaspoons …

OLD JOE   (*examining them*) Nice! Very nice indeed. Little hole in this one, but nothing that a little stitch or two couldn't hide, eh?

MRS FILCH   There's a couple of nice boots there.

OLD JOE   Pairs?

MRS FILCH   Course they're pairs! What's he gonna do with one? Hop?

OLD JOE   I don't suppose he'll be hopping anywhere anytime soon. Or walking for that matter.

MRS FILCH   Not the way we left him. He wouldn't have a stitch to wear.

They laugh grotesquely. All stopping with racking coughs.

MRS FILCH   *Now I've said it for a thousand times if I have said it once*
I'm a gentle soul who wouldn't hurt a fly
Though they say I'm soft and tender
I would gladly go and spend a
Night in hell to watch that bugger really fry

OLD JOE   *There's a saying for the knowing*
We all reap what we are sowing
There are better souls than him to try to save
So I couldn't give a tuppence
Now the bloke's got his comeuppance
We can have a good old knees up on his grave

MRS FILCH   *There'll be dancing*
Throughout the town

MRS DILBER   *When the undertaker's gone and nailed the blighter down*

ALL   *Just dessert, Just desserts*
We've hit the skinflint where it really hurts

> *Toodle-oo and bon voyage-ee*
> *There'll be no more argy-bargy*
> *No more debts*
> *See what he gets*
> *It's just desserts*

OLD JOE   All right, Mrs Dilber, time to get to yours.

MRS DILBER   He never made me rich when he was alive. Maybe the old goat can make amends now he's kicked the bucket.

OLD JOE   We'll see. We'll see.

MRS DILBER   Here, grab hold of this.

Mrs Dilber gets Old Joe to hold on to her skirt. She pirouettes laughing and what appeared to be her overskirt unravels to produce large bed curtains.

OLD JOE   (*laughing*) Mrs Dilber, you've done it again. A woman after me own heart.

MRS DILBER   Bed curtains.

OLD JOE   You don't mean you took 'em down, rings an' all, with him lying there?

MRS DILBER   I do. Them are the best money can buy.

OLD JOE   I'm sure they are, Mrs Dilber, I'm sure they are. 'Cepting you didn't buy 'em. There'll have to be a bit of discount there.

MRS DILBER   I got his blankets, too.

Mrs Dilber produces a bundle. Old Joe quickly unravels them.

OLD JOE   (*feeling the blankets*) You don't waste a minute, do you, Mrs Dilber? Still warm.

MRS DILBER   The only bit of warmth he ever gave us.

MRS DILBER   *I'm a very wholesome honest gal, as pure as driven snow*
Though in my time I've done me share of snatching
I knew where he was heading
When I stripped him of his bedding

OLD JOE   *Hope he didn't die of anything that's catching*

MRS FILCH *Well, it fills me heart with wonder*
Mrs Dilber, what a plunder!
Blankets, sheets and pillows, nearly got the set

MRS DILBER *Well, I know just 'ow to bleed 'em*
Where he's going he won't need 'em
He'll be warm enough where he is, you can bet

BOTH WOMEN *Say goodbye-ee*
Make a toast
He's invited to the feast but as the Sunday Roast

ALL *Just desserts, just desserts*
We've hit the skinflint where it really hurts
Now we know that it's for certain
He's rung down the final curtain
Take a bow
We must allow
It's just desserts
Just desserts, just desserts
We've hit the skinflint where it really hurts
And I'd say it to his face now
That the world's a better place now
That the villain's
Gone and got his
Just desserts
Just desserts!

Laughing, the three trundle the cart away as Scrooge and the Ghost of Christmas Yet to Come watch on. Ground mist starts to gather ...

MUSIC SCENE 16A

... and we hear the sound of a distant bell. The wind whistles about them. Gravestones appear around them growing and looming. The spirit points towards a small figure crouched near one particular stone. Bob Cratchit is kneeling at one. A small crutch is leaning against the tombstone. The inscription reads 'Our Beloved Tiny Tim'. Scrooge approaches at a distance.

SCROOGE No, spirit, please, say it isn't true.

BOB (*talking to the grave, softly*) And there's a pudding, Tim. Such a pudding. Just how you liked. Mother is preparing it as we speak. Look, you can see the spires of London from here, Tim, and hear the Christmas bells ring out. (*breaking down, unable to hold back the tears*) Oh, Tim, my boy, my boy.

Martha enters with her father's muffler. She stops to see her father.

MARTHA Father!

BOB (*wiping his eyes, quickly, so as not to show his grief*) Martha, my dear.

MARTHA (*coming close and wrapping his muffler around his shoulders*) Mother sent me to bring you home. She is worried you'll catch a cold on your chest.

BOB (*clasping her hands*) You're a good girl, Martha. See how London is bright this Christmas time. Tim can see everything from here.

MARTHA Yes. (*Pause*) The morning is cold, Father, and your hands are like ice. You have been out for so long. Come home.

BOB I don't like to think of Tim alone. He is so small.

MARTHA I know, Father.

BOB It is strange, but I feel him beside me, comforting me. A touch, Martha. His tiny hand in mine. Oh, Martha! My boy, my poor dead boy!

Bob breaks down once more and Martha comforts him as they slowly walk away. (Music Cue 16a has faded by now) A coffin is borne on by some ragged men. Slowly it passes them.

SCROOGE The poor child! The poor, poor child!

MUSIC CUE 16B

A tombstone, with a large skeletal statue on its plinth, moves towards Scrooge and Christmas Yet to Come. The bearers lower the coffin into the grave below it. They move off.

SCROOGE   Spectre, something tells me we are soon to part. Tell me, what man have we seen lying dead here? What creature has given so little to this world that no man can speak kindly of him?

The Spirit moves toward the grave pointing. Scrooge stands at a distance reluctant to move.

SCROOGE   Spirit, before I draw nearer to that stone, answer me one question; are these the shadows of things that must be or are they only those things that might be? I know that there are things that we cannot change unless the paths we choose are different. Will these shadows you have shown remain unchanged? Say that I can change them.

The spirit points once more to the grave. Scrooge creeps forward slowly. The tombstone, which has been blank until now, with a strange otherworldly scratching, starts to show the words that are being etched there. As Scrooge sees the letters become more distinct he falls slowly to his knees. The icy words read 'Ebenezer Scrooge'. As the last letter is inscribed, the skeletal figure on the tombstone suddenly opens vast black angel wings with a frightening whoosh of dry as dust flesh. Scrooge fall prostrate in absolute terror.

SCROOGE   No, spirit, no, no, no. Tell me I am not already dead! Tell me I am not already dead!

Scrooge pleads with the spirit, holding its robe.

Music Scene 16b is fading

Spirit, hear me, I am not the man I was. Believe me, I can change. Why show me all this if I am past all hope? Pity me, spirit! Give me the time to show you I can be a better man! I'll make good the wrongs! Oh, tell me I may sponge away the writing on this stone! Live a better life! Be the man I can be!

MUSIC CUE 17. TURN BACK THE CLOCK – SCROOGE

As the song progresses, the graveyard disappears and the spirit falls away to darkness.

SCROOGE   **Turn back the clock**
Give me strength to know I'm ready to
Turn back the clock
All the time that I have wasted

In my blindness
Human kindness was a thing I never saw
Turn back the clock
Forgive the man I was and please
Turn back the clock
And let my life be different
From the life I live
And please forgive the life I led before
A life that's oh, so very short
The life of mortal men
I'll learn the lessons that I've been taught
Begin my time again
The hands of time
Flow swiftly when you're older
And the hands of time
Can make the world seem colder
But a tiny spark
Can thaw the frost that grows within your heart
Let's make a start
I'll take my chances if I can
Turn back the clock
All the people who despised me
I will make amends
To all the friends I hope to grow to love
This has to be
A way for my salvation
I have got to see
It's time for reclamation
And that moment when
I'm born again
I'll find the courage, solid as a rock
Day by day
Let me learn
And I'll turn back the clock

The lights fade to darkness. We hear the Christmas morning bells pealing and as the lights come upon a bright new day, Scrooge is back in his bedchamber on the floor grasping the covers of the bed to him.

SCROOGE   Tell me I am not already dead! I will live a better life! I will be a better man … I will … I will …

He wakes with a start. He stares about him. He looks at his hands.

I'm alive. I'm alive. There are my hands, wonderful hands. Ten fingers. All there.

He wiggles them in front of his face, laughing. He clasps his arms around himself. He feels his face.

I'm alive. Kind spirits! Generous spirits! Caring, thoughtful, delightful spirits! My eyes are open! I will honour Christmas in my heart and try to keep it all the year. I will live in the past, the present and the future. The spirits of all three shall strive within me. I will not shut out the lessons they teach. Oh, Jacob Marley! Heaven and Christmas be praised for this! I say it on my knees, Old Jacob, on my knees.

Scrooge grabs at his bed curtains.

They're not torn down; they're not torn down, rings and all. They've not been sold. They are here. I am here. I can change the things I have seen. I know I can. I will change them.

Scrooge almost skips about the room.

Ah, the dear old bedpost. Good morning, bedpost. (*He kisses it, laughing*) There's where dear old Marley came in. That's where the Ghost of Christmas Present sat! It's all here! It's all true! It all happened! I don't know what day it is! I don't know how long I've been gone! I don't know anything. I'm quite a baby. Ha! Ha! Never mind! I don't care. I'm as merry as a schoolboy, I'm as light as a feather! A Merry Christmas! A Merry Christmas to all who can hear.

Scrooge laughs heartily and skips about. Mrs Dilber and Mrs Filch enter with clean sheets. They stare at him in fear.

MRS DILBER   Oh, my dear Lord! I think he's having a funny turn!

SCROOGE   (*swinging each in turn*) Dear ladies! Dear, dear ladies! What a beautiful morning! What a beautiful day! By the way, what day *is* it?

MRS FILCH   Why, it's Christmas day, sir.

SCROOGE   Then I haven't missed it!

MRS DILBER   Missed it?

SCROOGE   The spirits have done it all in one night. They can do anything they like. Of course they can. Of course they can. Clever spirits! Benevolent spirits!

MRS DILBER   Are you all right, sir?

SCROOGE   All right? All right? I have never been better, bless my soul! Mrs Dilber! Dear Mrs Filch! Something has happened! Something wonderful! Something spectacular! I'm happy! I can truly say I'm happy.

MRS DILBER   Shall I fetch the doctor, sir?

SCROOGE   Fetch my coat. I'm going out.

MRS FILCH   Like that, sir? You'll catch your death.

MRS DILBER   What'll the neighbours say?

SCROOGE   They'll say there goes a man who knows the true meaning of Christmas!

MRS DILBER   I'm fairly sure they won't.

SCROOGE   Then they'll come to know it.

MUSIC CUE 18. THE MAN IS MAD – SCROOGE, MRS DILBER & MRS FILCH

So much to do, so little time.

MRS DILBER   (*To Filch*) I think he's gone batty.

SCROOGE   *I've an unfamiliar feeling, one that sets the senses reeling*
And I haven't felt that feeling in a while
For it's spreading cross my face, just a glimmer, just a trace
It's a smile, dear Lord, it really is a smile
I can feel the muscles stretching and it's really rather fetching
Is this happiness I feel from deep within?

> *And I really must confide a smile that's slightly getting wider*
> *Almost surely must become a little grin*
> *Look at me, I'm fairly grinning, and I know it's the beginning*
> *Of a whole new world that's filled with joy and bliss*
> *Oh, this feeling is outrageous and I know that it's contagious*
> *Mrs Dilber, come and have a little kiss*

MRS DILBER   I'd rather have a shilling.

SCROOGE   You shall have that, too.

Scrooge chases the women round the room.

DILBER/FILCH   *He's gone mad!*

SCROOGE   *Ho! Ho! Ho!*

DILBER/FILCH   *The man is mad*

SCROOGE   *Hee! Hee! Hee!*

DILBER/FILCH   *All this gladness is just madness*
He's gone mad

SCROOGE   *Ha! Ha! Ha!*

DILBER/FILCH   *I'll say this, me dear old cocker,*
He's completely off his rocker
It's no joke, the barmy bloke's completely mad.

SCROOGE   *Ha! Ha! Ha!*
I could fill the air with laughter and live happy ever after
Doing all the things I know I have to do
I have joy enough to share, I could fairly dance on air
And I'm ready to begin the world anew
I'm as merry as a lark, I'll go skating in the park
Or perhaps I'll climb the very nearest tree
I'm as happy as an angel, this considerable change'll
Be the making of the man that I can be
They will say there goes a man who will do all he says he can do
I'll be busy as the bees are in their hive
Spreading cheer for those who need it, I shall do it, and God
speed it
And you'll see I'm quite the happiest man alive

DILBER/FILCH   *(in counterpoint) He's gone mad*
The man is mad
All this gladness is just madness
He's gone mad
I'll say this, me dear old cocker
He's completely off his rocker
It's no joke, the barmy bloke's completely mad

SCROOGE   *I'm not mad, my dear old lovelies; could you pass my hat and gloves please?*
What you see is just a man who's wide awake
All unhappiness is over and I feel I'm in the clover
I'll be generous and good for goodness sake

MRS DILBER   *Pinch me, am I really dreaming?*

MRS FILCH   *He's been at the gin, he's steaming!*
Or he may be stricken with a bout of flu

MRS DILBER   *Or he just might be doo-lally, for he's never been so pally*
But I like the man much better

MRS FILCH   *I do too (there is an orchestral fanfare)*

THREE   *After all this consternation, it's a time for celebration*
Let the bells ring out with joyous festive sound
There's a change in Mister Scrooge and that change is fairly huge
He's the happiest man I've seen in London town

SCROOGE   *I will strive*

DILBER/FILCH   *He will strive*

SCROOGE   *To keep Christmas in my heart where it will thrive*

DILBER/FILCH   *It will thrive*

SCROOGE   *From Pall Mall to North of Ealing*
I will spread this cheerful feeling

THREE   *And they'll say, here comes the happiest man alive!*

The women follow Scrooge over the gantry and into the street as the bed moves off.

ALL   *Here he comes*
             That cheery chappy
             Making all around him happy
             They will smile and they will shout it
             For there'll be no doubt about it
             He's the cheeriest chappy that's the happiest man alive!

The bells ring out. Scrooge gives the women some coins and they look to each other astonished and start to laugh. They run to tell the passers-by.

SCROOGE   What a beautiful morning! Ah, the bells! What music! Merry Christmas! Merry Christmas!

A small boy, the one who sang at Scrooge in Act I, is running by. Scrooge grabs him. The boy in terror looks up at Scrooge.

BOY   I ain't done it. Whatever it is, I ain't done it!

SCROOGE   Calm down, my fine fellow!

BOY   'Ere, it's you, isn't it? Let me be! I ain't bin singing nowhere near you!

SCROOGE   Do you want to earn yourself a shilling, my little buck?

BOY   Cor, would I!

SCROOGE   Do you know the butcher's in the next street but one?

BOY   The one on the corner?

SCROOGE   The very same. Clever boy! Excellent fellow! Do you know whether they've sold the prize turkey that was hanging up there?

BOY   The one as big as me?

SCROOGE   What a delightful boy! It's a pleasure to talk to him! Yes, my little fellow.

BOY   It's hanging there now.

SCROOGE   Is it? Go and buy it.

BOY   Can't see it happening, myself!

The boy makes to leave.

SCROOGE I am in earnest, my boy! Tell the man that I will pay whatever it costs. Here's a shilling and if you're back with that turkey in less than five minutes, I'll give you half a crown.

The boy is off like a shot as Scrooge laughs. Sam Billikin walks on and immediately seeing Scrooge turns on his heels to walk straight back off. Scrooge seeing this stops him.

Samuel Billikin!

SAM You've given me an extra week, don't forget, Mr Scrooge!

SCROOGE An extra week, is it?

SAM You did, Mr Scrooge, on my honour. Just last night. I have an extra week to pay at the cost of … er … one shilling extra.

SCROOGE One shilling? I'm sure it was two, Mr Billikin!

SAM Yes, yes, of course it was.

SCROOGE Hmm!

Scrooge takes out his notepad and pencil. He flicks through it.

SAM My business won't take much more. Don't say you're changing the terms, Mr Scrooge.

SCROOGE I am, Mr Billikin, I am. You will pay me what is due … on the twelfth of never.

SAM I can't … (*Suddenly realising what Scrooge has said*) You what?

SCROOGE The debt is cancelled, Sam. Merry Christmas!

SAM Cancelled? Are you quite all right, sir?

SCROOGE Never been better.

SAM Blimey! Merry Christmas, Mr Scrooge. And many more of them, I'm sure. I'm indebted to you, Mr Scrooge.

SCROOGE Not any more, Sam, not any more. And the same goes for the rest of you, all debts are wiped clean.

MUSIC CUE 19. FINALE

General Note. See vocal score for correct finale progression and adjust underscores with repeats, if necessary, to cover dialogue as written in the libretto during the finale.

Mr Ebenezer Scrooge wishes you all the joy of the season.

As the crowd assembled shout their approvals, Scrooge tears the pages from the book and throws them into the air.

SCROOGE *Good things come*
To those who wait

CAST *No matter who from me and you to heads of state*
But all I know
This much is true
That all the good things now are bundled up in you

The small boy returns, completely obscured by the turkey that is, in fact, as big as he is. We see nothing but the turkey.

SCROOGE *(laughing heartily)* What's this? The turkey has risen from the dead and walks to the dinner table itself!

The boy's head pops up above it.

BOY It's a whopper, innit?

SCROOGE You're right, my boy, it is, as you say, a whopper! And here's your half crown!

Scrooge takes the turkey from him and swings it round.

A glorious bird! A magnificent bird! Won't Bob Cratchit be happy to have you, my fine plump darling!

Scrooge dances with it as though with a waltz partner.

SCROOGE *When you are near*
My world's complete
And ev'ry minute with you in it is a treat
These moments come
And all too few
But they're enough when you have me and I have you

CAST   *Now, lighter than a feather*
        We're a happy band of laughing cavaliers
        When we are all together
        We have love to guide us all throughout the years

The two charitable gentlemen, Dickens being one, pass. Quick as a flash, Scrooge hands the turkey to an astonished gentleman near him and runs towards the charitable men.

SCROOGE   Gentlemen, a moment, if you will!

The gentlemen stop and eye him suspiciously. Scrooge takes hold of their hands in turn and shakes them vigorously.

        My dear sir, good morning, good morning!

DICKENS   Mr Scrooge?

SCROOGE   That is my name, and I fear it does not give you joy to hear it. Considering our last meeting, I don't think it should. No, indeed. But allow me to ask your pardon, sirs. I have a little business with you I feel sure.

DICKENS   Business with us?

SCROOGE   Those who are in need at this time of the year. I wish to offer my help. Something to the tune of …

Scrooge whispers in his ear. The Gentleman looks astonished. He whispers to the other.

GENTLEMAN#2   Lord Bless me! That is indeed generous! My dear Mr Scrooge, are you quite serious?

SCROOGE   If you please, not a farthing less. A great many back-payments are included in it, I assure you. Will you do me the favour of accepting?

DICKENS   On behalf of the needy, sir, I accept whole-heartedly.

The gentlemen stand dazed by Scrooge's generosity.

DRINK IT IN

SCROOGE   *Taste the Christmas flavour; let it season all you do*
        Sprinkle joy and laughter, come what may

THE GENTLEMEN *Life is more than pennies and the interest you accrue*
What is money but a thing to give away?

SCROOGE *Friendship makes you wealthy*

THE GENTLEMEN *Money brings just tears*
How will you be remembered in the coming years?

CAST *Drink it in*

SCROOGE *Don't be languid, limp and listless*

CAST *Drink it in*

SCROOGE *Take a draft of Merry Christmas*

CAST *Lift a glass and feel the spirit warm the cockles of the heart*

SCROOGE *Ancient grudges and ill feeling; set the silly things apart*

ALL *For the season of goodwill and love is just about to start*
Drink it in! Drink it in! Drink it in!

During the previous verse Scrooge runs to the gentlemen who he saddled with the turkey and retrieves it. Scrooge makes his way to the Cratchits' front door. He bangs hard. He puts on his old demeanour, laughs to himself, and bids the followers to hide. He bangs the door once more. He becomes the grim old Mr Scrooge.

Underscoring the next is **Do as the Cratchits Do**

SCROOGE (*harsh*) Cratchit! Bob Cratchit!

The door opens and Bob is there. He looks both astonished and frightened.

BOB Mr Scrooge, sir!

SCROOGE Why were you not at work this morning, sir?

BOB It's Christmas Day, sir. You gave me the day ...

SCROOGE Step this way, sir. I think I need a strong word or two with you.

Bob follows out onto the street. Mrs Cratchit comes to the door. She looks angry at the treatment of her husband. The children come spilling out after her.

BOB It's only once a year, Mr Scrooge. It shall not be repeated ...

SCROOGE	Now I will tell you what, my friend, I will not stand for this any longer …
MRS CRATCHIT	(*squaring up to him*) Now, you look here, Mr Scrooge …
SCROOGE	No, you look here, Mrs Cratchit … Ha! Ha! Look here … Oh, this really is too delicious …
MRS CRATCHIT	I'll not stand for anymore of this.
BOB	My dear!
MRS CRATCHIT	No, I'm going to give him a piece of my mind. Let me tell you, Mr High and Mighty Scrooge, my husband has slaved for you for years without ever a thank you and on a pittance …
SCROOGE	Well, well, I should think we will need to do something about that then, shouldn't we? Bob, I am about to…raise your salary!
MRS CRATCHIT	And another thing … (*Suddenly realising*) Raise his what?
SCROOGE	Double it, in fact. Merry Christmas, Bob! A merrier Christmas, Bob, than I have given you in many a year, my good fellow. And we shall start by getting this merry little family of yours whatever it needs for this special day. Starting with this!

The boy steps forward with the turkey as the others creep from their hiding places. Tim hobbles forward.

TIM	Why, it's the butcher's prize turkey!
SCROOGE	Wrong, my young fellow, it's *your* prize turkey!
MRS CRATCHIT	Whatever shall we do with our little goose?
SCROOGE	You can use it to stuff this! Ha! Ha! And as for you, my boy, what say you to the present of your choice? All you children, come help me pick something out!
PETER	Can we, Mama? Can we?
SCROOGE	(*aside to Bob*) And Bob, we shall find the best doctors for Tiny Tim, shan't we? The best doctors money can buy! We'll make him well again, just you wait and see.

BOB	Thank you, Mr Scrooge, thank you.
SCROOGE	Come then, Tim, let's go on a hunt for Christmas.
TIM	It's here already.
SCROOGE	Then, let us celebrate. You can show me how.

Scrooge lifts Tim onto his shoulder.

CHRISTMAS CHEER

ALL *Ring out the bells of love and laughter*
Joy has no equal here
Pealing for now and ever after
Chiming forth the Christmas cheer
Deck out the hall with all the jollity and joking and jest
Fill ev'ry stocking with a shocking lot of love and the rest
Let us be cheery 'stead of weary, 'stead of gloomy and glum
Come raise a glass to present, past and all the things yet to come
Goodwill, peace on earth to
All those far or near
All this I would wish you
Wrapped up in this Christmas cheer

Fred enters and Scrooge sees him.

SCROOGE	Fred!
FRED	Uncle Scrooge!
SCROOGE	Forgive an old man his folly! I beg your forgiveness.
FRED	You have done nothing to be forgiven for.
SCROOGE	Oh, I have. I have. All these years! All these wasted years! Do you think there might be another place at your table tonight for an old sinner like me? It *is* Christmas, and I think I should like to spend it with my family.

Scrooge holds out his hand to Fred in handshake and, instead of shaking it, Fred gives Scrooge a hug that wipes clean the years. Slowly Scrooge's arms close about him.

SCROOGE   (*looking up*) Old Marley, Dear Old Marley, I pledge this to you – I will keep Christmas in my heart now and always. I will live, Marley, I will live.

Dickens steps forward.

DICKENS   Scrooge was better than his word. He did it all and infinitely more. He became as good a friend, as good a master, and as good a man as the good old city knew, or any other good old city, town or borough in the good old world. And it was always said of him that he knew how to keep Christmas well. May that be truly said of all of us! And so, as Tiny Tim observed …

TINY TIM   God Bless us everyone!

ALL   God Bless us everyone!

ALL   *Here's a Christmas wish*
           To all who you hold dear
           Make this time delic- (delish)
           -ious laden down with Christmas Cheer
           One last time, (shouting) let's shout it
           Sing out, let us hear
           We won't go without it
           Very Merry Christmas Cheer
MEN   *Very Merry Christmas Cheer*

WOMEN   *Very Merry Christmas*

MEN   *Very Merry Christmas*

WOMEN   *Very merry, very merry*

MEN   *Very merry, very merry*

ALL   *Very Merry Christmas Cheer*
           Very Merry Christmas Cheer

Snow begins to fall as the music rises to its climax and the curtain falls.

END OF ACT II

MUSIC CUE 20. BOWS

After the final curtain…

MUSIC CUE 21. PLAYOUT